How to Think Critically

Question, Analyze, Reflect, Debate.

By Albert Rutherford

Copyright © 2021 by Albert Rutherford. All rights reserved.

No part of this publication may be reproduced, stored in a retrieval system, or transmitted in any form or by any means, electronic, mechanical, photocopying, recording, scanning or otherwise, except as permitted under Section 107 or 108 of the 1976 United States Copyright Act, without the prior written permission of the author.

Limit of Liability/ Disclaimer of Warranty: The author makes no representations or warranties with respect to the accuracy or completeness of the contents of this work and specifically disclaims all warranties, including without limitation warranties of fitness for a particular purpose. No warranty may be created or extended by sales or promotional materials. The advice and recipes contained herein may not be suitable for everyone. This work is sold with the understanding that the author is not engaged in rendering medical, legal or other professional advice or services. If professional assistance is required, the services of a competent professional person should be sought. The author shall not be liable for damages arising herefrom. The fact that an individual, organization of website is referred to in this work as a citation and/or potential source of further information does not mean that the author endorses the information the individual, organization to website may provide or recommendations they/it may make. Further, readers should be aware that Internet websites listed in this work might have changed or disappeared between when this work was written and when it is read.

For general information on the products and services or to obtain technical support, please contact the author.

Visit www.albertrutherford.com to claim your FREE GIFT: The Art of Asking Powerful Questions in the World of Systems

Table Of Contents

INTRODUCTION   1

CHAPTER 1: WHAT IS CRITICAL THINKING?   5

What does a Critical Thinker Look Like?   8

Benefits of Critical Thinking   11

CHAPTER 2: WHY IS CRITICAL THINKING SO CHALLENGING?   19

Noncritical, Weakly Critical, and Strongly Critical Thinking   21

The Linda Problem   33

The Problem with Eyewitness Accounts and Memory   38

Bayesian Analysis   41

CHAPTER 3: THE ESSENTIALS OF CRITICAL THINKING   49

The 7 Steps to Better Critical Thinking	49
The Universal Intellectual Standards	60
The Elements of Thinking	65
Valuable Intellectual Traits	73
CHAPTER 4: EMOTIONS, ASSUMPTIONS, AND BIASES	**81**
Moods and Thinking	83
The Science Behind our Biases	85
Jumping to Conclusions	90
Types of Biases	96
Marketing and Manipulation	106
How to Detect Biases in Data and Information	117
Minimize the Impact of Your Biases	123
CHAPTER 5: HOW TO UNDERSTAND MORE DEEPLY	**131**
Make Mistakes and Ask Questions	136

Asking Questions in Different Situations 144

Follow the Flow of Ideas and Embrace Change 149

CHAPTER 6: REASONING BY ANALOGY 155

The Power of Words 157

Uncovering False Analogies 164

Analogy in Practice 165

Reflection: Practice Your Analogy Skills 168

CONCLUSION 173

SUMMARY GUIDE 175

BEFORE YOU GO... 181

REFERENCES 183

Introduction

I first met the concept of critical thinking in my early thirties. Without entertaining you with how many centuries ago this encounter happened, let me tell you this: I thought I could never master this seemingly ungraspable way of thinking. When I heard the words "critical thinking," I imagined astute diplomats, cunning politicians, and other kinds of geniuses practicing it, taking advantage of the rest of us.

But I was approaching the art of critical thinking in a narrow-minded and uncritical fashion. It's not a secret cognitive practice reserved for a select few. In fact, everyone can learn to use critical thinking to their advantage if they are somewhat curious, creative, and clever. In other words, most of us can practice this type of thinking. Yet not so many of us do. My mission in this book is to unveil the mystery of critical thinking and help you adopt its basic principles.

Before I engage in the presentation of the nitty gritty, please read the following statements and decide if you'd like to become better at doing each or any of them.

- Interpret others' needs by assessing their behavior, words, and body language and offer them proper help or support.
- Settle arguments as objective as possible by validating each party and

presenting alternative, fair solutions to each party.
- Organize ideas for an essay, story, or news article, paying attention to the complexities of the motivation of each character—real or fictional.
- Gather and analyze data with precision and conduct valid experiments.
- Based on data, assess and anticipate consequences of various decisions and take action to mitigate their negative impacts—for example, in your business.
- Scrutinize your or your competitors' strengths and weaknesses to optimize your strategies.
- See through marketing schemes and be an informed customer.
- Ask clever questions for new insights.

- Investigate, examine, and evaluate information to reach more accurate conclusions.
- See yourself in a more objective way and use this knowledge to present your skills in a relevant and advantageous way at, for example, job interviews.

Strong critical-thinking skills will help you do better in the areas mentioned above and more. And this book will tell you how to develop those skills. Without further ado, let's start our journey!

Chapter 1: What is Critical Thinking?

At its core, critical thinking is the ability to look at things logically, to put together to form judgments and make decisions.

Critical thinking was popularized in the "Critical Thinking Movement" of the 1980s, which was born from the belief that the rote memorization methods in schools were not the best way to teach students. Instead, the movement suggested that children learn better when they can be hands-on, learning by doing and discovering concepts themselves. From that point onward, education became not just about imparting information through incantations and repetition and expecting it to be absorbed, but about teaching the students how to find their own connections and meaning from lessons, making them active participants in the process of learning rather than just recitation machines. The results were improved long-term memorization and strengthened skills that would be valuable for employers, ensuring that students graduated not just with knowledge but with the tools to build that comprehension even further and grow and learn for the rest of their lives.

Clearly, the movement was on to something, as the evolution to schooling was lasting and remains apparent in education even today, showing no signs of going out of style anytime soon. From teachers to business executives and political leaders, most people continue to see critical thinking as an essential skill that students need in order to be successful in the workplace and in life.[1] But some people are much better at it than others.

Those who look at solving problems with hard facts and statistics, who listen to people's wild stories with a critical ear, who fact-check and source their material, and who ask frequent questions are good critical thinkers. These people are stronger at debating because they come up with evidence that is harder to argue against and are more willing to look at another viewpoint or be impartial because they take advice from all sides before deciding their own opinion. They never go with just their "gut feeling" and rarely act on their emotions.

---

[1] Insight Assessment. Expert Consensus on Critical Thinking. Insight Assessment. 2018.
https://www.insightassessment.com/Resources/Importance-of-Critical-Thinking/Expert-Consensus-on-Critical-Thinking

And they're always researching and asking questions to get to the bottom of things.

What does a Critical Thinker Look Like?

Although critical thinking can present itself in many ways, there are three tell-tale signs of a good critical thinker:

1. A certain skepticism

> A healthy dose of skepticism is necessary for being a good critical thinker because it ensures you don't just deny or accept things at face value but instead wait to gather more information or hear the other

side of the story. This isn't necessarily about disbelieving people and what they tell you but opening your mind to the possibility that they have a limited view or biases that they might not even know are skewing their facts.

2. A natural curiosity

Curiosity may have killed the cat, but satisfaction brought it back. Likewise, critical thinkers are always seeking more information and greater understanding, continuing to dig deeper until they are satisfied that they have an honest and true answer. Good critical thinkers will often find themselves studying topics that were mentioned in conversations they had earlier in the day, asking a lot of follow-up questions to a story, and diving into the details of things they hear about in their day-to-day lives. They are students of life who love the pursuit of knowledge.

3. Humility

Critical thinkers have an open mind and are willing to accept the perspectives of others even if they go against their own. They prize being factual over being right and they don't see debate as a win-lose game but a way to get an answer or come to a conclusion. They don't cling blindly to their beliefs but are willing to accept new evidence and allow it to shape their judgment.[2]

Benefits of Critical Thinking

Critical thinking may conjure up ideas of classroom exercises and academic research. It may seem like a formal skill used only for poking holes in claims and debating. But it's far more practical than that. Critical thinking allows you to make informed decisions, to recognize what is morally right or wrong and what is honest and true. Being a good critical

---

[2] Frank, T. What is Critical Thinking? - Definition, Skills & Meaning. Study. 2018.
http://study.com/academy/lesson/what-is-critical-thinking-definition-skills-meaning.html

thinker also means you have a penchant for analysis, an openness to accept new knowledge, and an insatiable desire for deeper understanding, whether that's deciphering what news sources are correct, finding the lowest price for the sweater you've been eyeing, or deciding what career path is best for achieving your life goals.

Thinking critically can improve your life in so many areas. Research has shown that those who are better critical thinkers can make connections between ideas in ways that other people cannot and judge the importance and significance of ideas more easily.[3] They are also more efficient at identifying quality arguments and evidence and can find errors in reasoning, whether it be their own or others,

---

[3] Thinking, Critical. An Interview with Linda Elder About Using Critical Thinking Concepts and Tools. Critical Thinking. 2002. https://www.criticalthinking.org/pages/an-interview-with-linda-elder-about-using-critical-thinking-concepts-and-tools/495

making them more likely to succeed and less apt to grow frustrated by challenges.

Critical thinking can even promote creativity because it teaches you the importance of thinking in new ways and relying on the power of your own mind rather than accepting things as they are. Also, it relies on questioning ideas and looking at the bigger picture, which are often a part of the artistic process.

Reflection: Are You a Critical Thinker?

Use these questions to reflect on how you react when faced with problems. Make sure to be honest with yourself (no one's listening!).

- Do you take into account alternative solutions and opinions even when they go against something you believe?
- Do you have a natural curiosity?
- Do you enjoy learning new things?

- Do you consider yourself to be a lifelong learner who enjoys seeking out new knowledge?
- Are you confident in your reasoning skills?
- Do you wait to pass judgment until you have all the facts?
- Do you keep an open mind when it comes to differing viewpoints?
- Are you understanding of others' ideas and opinions?
- Do you try to be fair and impartial when assessing evidence?
- Are you aware of and honest about your biases, stereotypical thinking, and prejudices?
- Are you willing to go where the facts take you even if it means changing or dismissing previously held opinions?

- Are you able to create quality questions and identify problems accurately?
- Are you good at gathering, evaluating, and interpreting new information?
- Do you take the time to make sure the answers you find are correct and of high quality rather than just relying on them being an answer to a given solution?
- Do you recognize your own biases and that of others and try your best to overcome them?
- Can you effectively communicate your ideas and questions to others in a way that allows them to help you find answers and build off your ideas?[4]

---

[4] Thinking, Critical. Critical Thinking: Where to Begin. Critical Thinking. 2017.
http://www.criticalthinking.org/pages/critical-thinking-where-to-begin/796

If you can honestly answer yes to a majority of these questions on most days, then you just might be a critical thinker. But that doesn't mean this book can't help you. As you may already know, critical thinking is an ongoing process and can always be improved.

If you answered no, don't worry! By picking up this book you've already shown a natural curiosity and taken your first step on the right path to improving your reasoning. In the following sections, we'll explore some concepts for achieving deeper understanding and methods to upgrade your reasoning skills developed by some of the greatest minds on the topic.

No matter how critical of a thinker you are (or aren't), there are a few practical tips and tricks that can help you start to build your skills. All you need is a willingness to put in the time and effort and take on the mentality of a lifelong learner who is open to new knowledge. No matter who you are or your current skill level, if you open your mind and practice enough, you can hone your critical-thinking abilities in a way that will make you more confident and enhance your quality of life.

Chapter 2: Why is Critical Thinking so Challenging?

Our minds are made to think, but the *way* they think can be altered with practice. Because stereotypes and biases are a way of shortcutting our thinking, our brains see them as the more efficient thought process and will rely heavily on them when left to their own devices. In comparison, research, skepticism, formulating questions, and other aspects of critical thinking take much more brain power and require our minds to work harder. To our minds, this is like deciding between going on a short walk or taking on a marathon. Obviously, the walk seems much more doable and less strenuous. But if we practice running enough, the marathon will not be that difficult. Likewise, if we work our critical-thinking muscles, our brain will find them more natural to use, and those longer paths will be worn in and made more accessible and welcoming. It takes a lot of effort to get to this point, just like it takes a lot of work to be able to run a marathon, but it will slowly become easier and easier with practice. Plus, the benefits are extraordinary; we can learn to break away from our biases and have a more open mind, allowing us to communicate and explore ideas rather than becoming stuck in the same old cycles of reasoning.[5]

---

[5] Thinking, Critical. Critical Thinking: Where to Begin. Critical Thinking. 2017.
http://www.criticalthinking.org/pages/critical-thinking-where-to-begin/796

Noncritical, Weakly Critical, and Strongly Critical Thinking

Critical thinking can be difficult because it's not black and white; good reasoning comes in varying degrees. Sometimes your approach (or another's) will be better than other times. But that's okay—*if* you can recognize the difference between a critical approach and a noncritical approach and be able to use your own critical-thinking energy wisely. Being a good critical thinker is about taking the multitude of opportunities you have in a day to use your reasoning and deduction skills and putting them to good use with the limited resources you have.

Our modern world is overpopulated with information bombarding us from all sides. It takes a shrewd eye to pick out which ones are critical and significant sources and which have little to offer. Realizing how critical you (or others) are being in a certain situation will allow you to understand what kind of conclusion you've come to or to establish how critical the material you're taking in is. Oftentimes, what appear to be good, critical arguments on the surface are really just noncritical or weakly critical reasoning marauding as something more thorough. Therefore, the first step to critical thinking is being able to acknowledge when evidence is flawed versus when it's strong, whether it's your own or that of material you're taking in.

Noncritical

A noncritical approach is to accept information at face value without question or challenge. This is usually how we address material given to us by a trusted source who we assume we can put our faith into. But it can also occur when we agree with the opinions being stated or when the explanation makes sense to us and leads to logical-sounding conclusions. For example, we may read a news article and accept that the basis and statements of the piece are in line with reality because we assume news articles are inherently well-researched and objective. Because of this, we don't look deeper into any inaccuracies or biases that may or may not exist.

The problem with noncritical thinking is that it often relies on feelings and emotions rather than facts. These senses can sometimes be so overwhelming that we take them as hard evidence. When we trust a friend's judgment, for instance, it's usually based on our relationship with them more than it's about their actual knowledge or skills. Yet we still see them as a reliable resource. Even if this friend is brilliant and often knows what they're talking about, it's a tricky situation to put your faith into someone so wholeheartedly; you may never perceive when and if they're wrong. It's important to remember that these feelings you have aren't tied to the information itself and don't necessarily make the claim true.

A noncritical source will trust too much in information that may not be reputable, often lean in a particular direction, and may not include much research or has poor research. The red flag of a noncritical source would be that it doesn't list other sources or takes all its data from one place or person or doesn't provide much original material or analysis.

Weakly Critical

A weakly critical approach addresses inaccuracies or incorrect conclusions while still accepting the main assumptions or concepts presented. Weakly critical means being wary but willing to accept the given statements. For example, being weakly critical of a new article would mean looking at any linked sources and background research used to see if it has been misconstrued or taken out of context and examining the partisanship and standing of the newsroom the article came from. You may find when you take a closer look that the arguments it poses are quite flimsy, such as by taking all its data from one source or not including much thorough background research.

To engage in a conversation with a trusted friend with a weakly critical approach you may ask where they heard their information from or how they know so much about a certain topic. Remember that you're not necessarily looking to disprove something but simply trying to look at how thorough that material is. Is it a file heaping with documents or a slim few bits of paper? Is it a textbook filled with small print or a leaflet? This will help you verify whether there's more you should look into or if the given data is sufficient. Skepticism, in a healthy amount, doesn't mean you're difficult to please or combative, but that you simply have the independence to make your own decisions. As Ronald Reagan often mentioned the rhyming Russian proverb: "Trust but verify."[6]

---

[6] Barton Swaim (11 March 2016). "'Trust, but verify': An untrustworthy political phrase". *The Washington Post*. Retrieved 25 June 2019.

A weakly critical source may be recognized by its minimal or limited research. In some cases, it may look like it has many sources, but these may come from the same place or from the same small group of people, who are likely biased. It may come to conclusions or contain analysis, but it is usually minimal or overgeneralized.

Strongly Critical

In this approach, the material is taken apart and examined from every angle, investigating every piece of it from the authority of the source to the soundness of every piece of evidence. Other research is also taken into account at this stage to reveal whether the stated stance is an outlier or is in agreement with others. Assumptions and biases are looked at and errors or weakness in reasoning are sought out, not only in the information itself but in others that it cites as sources.[7]

If you took a strongly critical approach to dissect a news article, you would look into the predilections of the media outlet and its standing and perhaps even those of the author. You would not only look at all the sources cited but also go a step further into doing your own research and seeing if the same results come up or if there are differing theories. You might find that quotes have been taken out of context, that statistics and data have been copied without being bothered to be analyzed, that facts have been (conveniently) left out, or that sources have been disproven. Or you could find that the piece checks out and,

---

[7] Thinking Writing. Non-Critical And Critical Approaches. Thinking Writing. 2018.
http://www.thinkingwriting.qmul.ac.uk/noncritical/critical

through your investigation, have an even greater understanding of the topic that you can use in the future.

To be strongly critical of a friend would mean that you ask follow-up questions and inquire with other people about their thoughts on the matter. You might even do your own research to verify what was said.

A strongly critical source will have a lot of analysis and research that comes from a variety of places and will have an objective stance. It will rely on facts more than opinions and will be verifiable by other sources.

Uncritical-illogical thinking

To be a good critical thinker, you must come to terms with the fact that we, as humans, often make mistakes in our reasoning and come to incorrect conclusions. But these errors can be predicted. Awareness of your propensities and common mistakes will strengthen your critical-thinking skills and make you less likely to blunder.

Psychologists have sorted these mistakes in reasoning into two major categories: "hot," or motivational illusions, and "cold," or cognitive illusions. "Hot" illusions are founded on feelings and emotions. These mistakes are often based on the assumption that the things we believe now we will always believe when, in truth, we're always growing and changing, and our thoughts can be altered quite drastically over the years. "Cold" illusions are errors in thinking, such as biases, mistakes in reasoning, or incorrectly identifying a problem.[8]

Unfortunately, both types are hardwired into our brains. Many experts believe this is because such jumps in reasoning allowed us to make quicker decisions in survival situations when time was of the essence. Although that is no longer the case, in some ways, these shortcuts can still be beneficial. Studies show that people who serve their own interests even when presented with contradictory evidence may achieve more in life and have greater motivation and productivity.[9] For example, students who flaunt their achievements on entrance exams may be more likely to receive a scholarship or be accepted into university even if they overestimated their abilities or overinflated their experiences.

---

[8] Correia, Vasco. Biases and fallacies: The role of motivated irrationality in fallacious reasoning. Vasco Correia. 2018. https://pdfs.semanticscholar.org/7f27/529ac93c3d86bd2b251d1787c63f0d10fb3c.pdf

[9] Biswas-Diener, Robert. Kashdan Todd B. What Happy People Do Differently? Psychology Today. 2013. https://www.psychologytoday.com/us/articles/201307/what-happy-people-do-differently

However, this tendency can too often lead to poor outcomes in the long run, resulting in decision-making and preparation errors because they feel that unfortunate circumstances and negative implications won't affect them. This attitude will also inflate their ego, making them feel superior to those around them in a way that can ostracize them and contribute to reestablishing biases and stereotypes. This will limit their viewpoint and make them less open to new information and experiences and less willing to take on new knowledge that will allow them to grow as a person.

The Linda Problem

The way our brain relies so heavily on assumptions and biases is a phenomenon that has been studied by experts in the field for decades. Slowly but surely, discoveries have been made that have allowed us to understand how to navigate them, such as that of the conjunction fallacy or the "Linda problem."

In 1983, psychology professors Amos Tversky and Daniel Kahneman conducted a study on unintentional bias by presenting a group of student participants with the following scenario:

"Linda is thirty-one years old, single, outspoken, and very bright. She majored in philosophy. As a student, she was deeply concerned with issues of discrimination and social justice, and also participated in anti-nuclear demonstrations."[10]

---

[10] Brogaard, Berit. PhD. Linda The Bank Teller Case Revisited. Psychology Today. 2016.
https://www.psychologytoday.com/us/blog/the-superhuman-mind/201611/linda-the-bank-teller-case-revisited

The professors then gave the students a choice between two possible statements that would apply to Linda to see whether they would draw on preconceived stereotypes to make their decision when given so little information:

1. Linda is a bank teller.
2. Linda is a bank teller and is active in the feminist movement.

Although nothing in the description would lead participants to believe Linda would be a bank teller, it had been written in a way that suggested she *would* be active in social justice—such as the feminist movement. But, for the second option to be true, the first must also be true. Statistically, two pieces of specific information are *always* less probable than just one, making the second choice mathematically less likely to be correct.

If that goes against your instinct (as it might), think of it this way: If you were asked the likelihood that you would be struck by lightning, you would probably say it's pretty rare. Right? But if you were asked the likelihood of being struck by lightning while being bitten by a shark, you would say it would be almost impossible. Both are very rare occurrences, so the likelihood they would both happen at the same time is so small it's almost nonexistent. Being a bank teller and a feminist are much more likely things to occur in day-to-day life, but they are still less likely to occur together because it relies on one already being true.

Yet, you probably found yourself leaning towards the second option, didn't you? You're not alone; 86% of participants chose option 2 as well. By combining a piece of information that was likely with one that had no foundation in truth whatsoever, Kahneman and Tversky confirmed the implicit error in the reasoning of human beings, showing the way our brains' tendency to try to save energy causes it to take shortcuts to come up with answers faster instead of doing the research and putting in the effort to calculate a conclusion.

When participants looked at the answers, their brain made the connection that being active in the feminist movement made sense with the description and had some relation. Therefore, their minds filled in the gaps and assumed that Linda *must* be a bank teller and chose the second option as it appeared to fit more specifically with the facts given even though there was nothing to back up that belief.

Those that didn't answer with the second option might have second-guessed this conjecture and took a second to ask themselves: "Where is this bank teller part coming from?" This question would lead them to see that there was no relevant connection. They may have even looked at it mathematically and found that the second option was statistically less probable than the first. However, this process would have taken longer and required a deeper level of thought, which the brain must be willing to participate in.

Like those who faced the Linda problem, most people rely on stereotypes to make decisions, even if they don't think they do. The brain loves to have these subconscious shortcuts as it's a much quicker and familiar way to do things. But they have the unfortunate trait of often being wrong. Critical thinkers take the time to become aware of what stereotypes and biases they rely on so they know when their brain is trying to do things the quick way and stop it from jumping to incorrect conclusions. This is a constant battle, but a necessary one if we want to have profound and objective analysis that allows for greater understanding and more truthful and factual results.

The Problem with Eyewitness Accounts and Memory

Not only does the brain like to pretend that our assumptions and emotions are good source material, it also tends to lead us to believe that its memory is more capable than it is. The longer it's been since an event has passed, the more likely it is that we'll see it as fact, even though it isn't. As we commit our experiences to memories, we deposit them into the Rolodex of our brains as a viable source of information. But, in reality, humans are lousy at remembering things. We can usually only grasp the "gist" of what happened. These interpretations can also be misconstrued or misinterpreted by ourselves or others.

Yet we still believe that eyewitness accounts are reliable sources. After all, they're used in court cases quite often. But these testimonies are only taken into account when they can be backed up by others. This is because two people can see the same thing and describe it in contrasting ways. This may simply be due to their view of the event or for a host of other reasons. For example, their opinions and biases could have altered their perspective on the matter, who they talked to about it afterward might have swayed their perception, or their feelings and emotions at the time might have affected their memory. Even if an eyewitness account is completely accurate (which is almost impossible), a person's story can also be easily misunderstood or can be tainted by the way it was produced through specifically worded questions or manipulation by an interviewer.

Still, that doesn't make eyewitness accounts completely worthless. When looked at in the right way and with the right tools and methods, such as Bayesian analysis, a lot can be gained from even such a partial account.

Bayesian Analysis

We often refer back to our emotional response as a form of fact, even when we know that the only reliable type of information is data and statistics. However, there is a strategy to combine both, allowing us to verify our experiences and interpretations with mathematical reasoning.

Probability and statistics are powerful tools for a critical thinker. When used correctly, they can create hard data to back up (or discredit) what would otherwise be shaky reasoning, allowing us to investigate our "hot" illusions for deeper truths. This can be achieved with what's called Bayesian analysis.

Bayesian analysis is a method of statistical inference that combines prior knowledge with evidence from a sample to guide research using probability in conjunction with real experiences, such as eyewitness accounts. For example, if a witness was asked to identify a car in a hit-and-run accident and said that the car was blue, Bayesian analysis could compare this new data with the likelihood of the car being blue to see the probability it would be correct.

By taking the number of cars in the city and calculating the percentages of each color it could be discovered how likely it was that the hit-and-run was caused by a blue car. For example, if 85% of cars in the city were green and 15% were blue, this would mean that a blue car would be less likely to be the culprit. Although this doesn't disprove the witness's statement, it does create greater context and clarity on the situation.

However, if the witness was tested on their ability to correctly identify colors, this could give even greater insight into their account of the situation. Let's say they took a test and discovered they could identify a car's color 80% of the time. That makes them incorrect 20% of the time. When combined with the probability that the car was blue, this makes the likelihood that the witness was incorrect much more probable. Although it still doesn't disprove their account, such calculations certainly change the level of confidence others might have in the witness's description.[11]

Bayesian theory follows the formula $P(H \cap D) = P(H|D)P(D) = P(D|H)P(H)$. This states that, given the two events of D (where D stands for data) and H (where H stands for hypothesis), the probability of D and H happening at the same time is the same as the probability of D occurring, given H, weighted by the P (probability) that H occurs, or vice versa.[12]

---

[11] Kahneman, Daniel. Thinking, Fast and Slow. Penguin. 2011.

[12] Mages Blog. Hit and run. Think Bayes! Mages Blog. 2014. https://magesblog.com/post/2014-07-29-hit-and-run-think-bayes/

Although this may just look like a bunch of PhDs, this method is extremely useful and isn't as complicated as it sounds. Let's break it down.

First, decide on your data and hypothesis. We know that our hypothesis is that the accident was caused by a blue car. You might want to say that the data is the percentage of blue cars in the city, as this gives a nice round number. But, in truth, the data is that the witness said that the car was blue because that is the baseline evidence.

Now all that's left to do is to input our calculations into the formula to replace the letters. P(H) becomes 15% for the 15% of cars that are blue in the city. P(D) refers to the probability of the data. In this case, that would be the likelihood that the witness's statement is true, or 80% as decided by the test that showed the witness could correctly identify the color 80% of the time.

When we put these into the formula we come up with:

$P(D) = P(D|H)P(H) + P(D|\bar{H})P(\bar{H}) = 0.8*0.15 + 0.2*0.85 = 0.29$

The witness was right 80% of the time, which, when multiplied by the 15% likelihood of the car being blue based on city statistics (0.15x0.80), results in a 12% chance that the car was blue.

But the unlikelihood must also be taken into account. In other words, there was an 85% chance the car was green and a 20% chance the witness would incorrectly identify the color (0.85x0.20) resulting in a 17% chance the car was green.

Adding this together (0.17+0.12), we come up with the result that the witness would identify the car as being blue 29% of the time, or 29 times out of every 100 accounts. However, this doesn't factor in whether the witness would be right or wrong. To figure that out, we'll need to take one more step.

Since the witness was correct 12% of the time, we can divide that likelihood by the number of occasions the witness would choose blue (0.12/0.29) and find that the witness would be correct in choosing blue 41% of the time.

Now we have an answer … sort of. This percentage can't tell us whether the witness is correct or not, only that they have a 41% chance of being correct. Even if there was only a 1% chance, it would still be possible that the one blue car in the city happened to be driving by and the witness took a shot in the dark despite being very bad at distinguishing colors and was correct. But, in that case, it would be very unlikely they were correct. This background research gives us a lot more context than if we had just taken the witness at their word. A 41% chance of being correct is fairly good, but not overwhelmingly positive, giving us some reason to doubt their account. This may mean we want to bring in more witnesses or look deeper at the facts than if they had, say, a 90% likelihood of being correct.

Reflection

Now that you have a more thorough understanding of what critical reasoning is and what it's not, take a look at something in your daily life, whether it's the story of a friend, a news article, a research paper, or some other material. Decide what your initial reaction to the material is, why you feel that way, and whether it's an emotional or logical response.

Do you trust your friend's account because it makes sense or because you react positively to them and want to trust them? Do you accept the statements of the research you've looked at because it's written formally (sounds smart) and was authored by someone with a lot of credentials or because the actual data and statistics back it up? Decide whether the material is noncritical, weakly critical, or strongly critical based on the things we've discussed, considering what can be verified and how.

Chapter 3: The Essentials of Critical Thinking

Because critical thinking is seen as such an essential skill and has been found to be so beneficial, it has been studied in-depth by experts in the field who have identified its main components. From this more easy-to-understand and simplified approach to the topic, several techniques have arisen.

The 7 Steps to Better Critical Thinking

Psychologists Carole Wade and Carol Tavris are two such experts, who became known for their contributions in bringing critical thinking into the world of psychology education. After years of research, the two came up with seven main facets that can be broken down into steps for improving your reasoning.[13]

Step 1. Question (Almost) Everything

Questioning things isn't just about pointing out what's wrong or disproving something, it's about learning more about it. Ask questions to get a deeper understanding, to uncover a new perspective, or to make new discoveries.

Questioning requires that you allow your mind to wander when information is posed, letting it

---

[13] Tarvis, Carole, and Carol Wade. *Psychology in Perspective,* 2nd ed. (Longman Publishers, 1997);Wade, Carole. Tavris, Carol. Gary, Marianne. Psychology, 5th ed. (Longman Publishers. 1998).

meander through possible streams of thought while trying to steer it towards new and unanswered theories. Then, consider:

- Why was this part of the problem or theory previously ignored?
- How did we end up where we are?
- What's wrong here?
- Why is this the way it is instead of another way?[14]

These questions will help to guide you in predicting whether a path of thought is worth pursuing or not.

Step 2. Articulate the Question[15]

---

[14] Wade, Carole. Tavris, Carol. Gary, Marianne. Psychology. Longman Publishers. 1998.
[15] Wade, Carole. Tavris, Carol. Gary, Marianne. Psychology. Longman Publishers. 1998.

Allowing your mind to probe an idea is one thing, but nailing down that idea and forming it into something fully developed is a whole other level of difficulty. Yet, it is a necessary step. Only by creating that question and actually posing it will you get answers.

Asking a question may seem simple but, if you're actually trying to get an accurate answer, it has to be done correctly. Human nature dictates that we try not to be proven wrong, subconsciously making us phrase inquiries in ways that urge others to agree with us or give us the response we're looking for. For example, "Can't we all agree that this is the right path forward?" will elicit a very different answer than "Do you think this is the right thing to do?"

Although agreement and predictability may be comfortable, they don't lead to many discoveries and optimal growth opportunities. You need to try to gather information rather than influence by avoiding words, changing tones, or body language. This is incredibly difficult, as you may not even be aware that you're unwittingly asking for agreement. But by reading these lines right now you're becoming more self-aware. Familiarize yourself with your tendencies of tweaking your inquiries. The earlier you get a handle on this, the better. You will gradually get a grasp on the works of your subconscious. You will be able to catch yourself when you're phrasing a question a particular way. Ask yourself, "What is my intention with this question? Do I seek agreement or do I seek the truth? How would I reply to my question? How could I phrase my question differently to avoid implying a desired answer?" The more you self-test your questions, the more adept you become at critical thinking. You'll learn more about how you think and act and why.

Step 3. Examine Evidence and Biases

Now that you've created your question, it's time to start answering it. Consider what goes against and what agrees with your argument while being cognizant of biases and assumptions. Biases are tricky because they may lead you to believe you've found an answer when, in reality, it rests solely on opinions or feelings rather than evidence. Biases are hard to address because they usually run so deep within our beliefs and experiences that we don't always notice when they emerge.

Not only do you have to worry about your own biases, but those inherent in the material we consume. Other people impart their biases all the time whether they realize it or not, a fact which must be taken into account when researching. From the stories told to us by friends to articles written by experts online, when we take in information, we must always be conscious of the lens it's being viewed through, whether it's our own or another's.

Step 4. Don't Let Emotional Reasoning Hold You Back

Not only can biases get in the way of allowing you to be a good critical thinker, but so can your emotions. It's hard to separate our feelings from a subject, but it must be done in order to get to the bottom of an issue. Going with an idea just because of your "gut" or believing in something just because you feel strongly about it isn't *wrong*, but it isn't critical. You must always ask yourself whether what you're looking at is a fact or a feeling. Too often the two will be intertwined and you'll have to extricate them. You must also do this with information others give you, who may not accept how their emotions are tied to their experiences and have muddled the facts, creating an impression of a situation that may not be rooted in the reality of what happened at all.

Step 5. Avoid Overgeneralization

Overgeneralizations are the enemy of critical thinking. They give the impression of having an answer but are really so vague or simplistic that they do nothing to solve the problem. A good critical thinker doesn't stop at level one, they continue climbing to get to the real insights so they can have the full picture of the situation. When we allow ourselves to achieve only the most obvious level of discovery, we close ourselves off to greater possibilities and discoveries. This goes against the core values of critical thinking, to be open and objective to interpreting information and to use reasonable judgments to find potential explanations and solutions to problems.

Step 6. Think Again

Just because you've found one answer doesn't mean it's the only one … or even the right one. You must resist the urge to accept easy judgments, even when they seem to be backed up by evidence. Go further and ask yourself what other explanations there could be. Try to step out of your own shoes and factor in other perspectives when doing this, taking into account how other people's opinions and sides of the story may factor into the overall picture and provide new comprehension. Consider whether the conclusions can be corroborated. Bringing in new material and observations will always make an argument more thorough.

Step 7. Accept Uncertainty

It's human nature to want to be right, to want to know everything. But good critical thinkers can escape this instinct and accept uncertainty because they know that it's not just about finding *an* answer but finding a *good* answer. When we have a problem or a question, we want to get to the bottom of it as quickly as possible to feel the relief that comes with a solution and move on with our lives. But the quickest way is not always (or even often) the most correct. Critical thinking takes the long way around, but it's worth it in the end to get to a better and more resolute destination. However, that journey takes a bit more patience and work and comes with a lot of uncertainty.

Even the best critical thinkers don't always find an answer, because not all questions have one. There may be multiple solutions, or it may be impossible to answer them at this period in time or with the information that's available. It may be impossible for you to solve it with your current know-how and skills but possible for someone else. Or there could be other issues that get in the way of finding a satisfying conclusion. Sometimes, the end result will simply be the acceptance that you don't know. But that's okay. It's about the journey, not the destination. Our brains hate uncertainty, but we can teach them to tolerate a bit here and there in the pursuit of knowledge. We just have to remind ourselves that, no matter what conclusions we do or don't come to, we'll always be sure to learn something if we put our critical thinking to use.

The Universal Intellectual Standards[16]

Dr. Richard Paul, the Director of Research and Professional Development at the Center of Critical Thinking and the former chair of the National Council for Excellence in Critical Thinking, has written numerous books on the subject that have garnered him world renown. His wife, Dr. Lina Elder, is also an accomplished expert in the field and an

---

[16] Elder, Linda. Paul, Richard. Universal Intellectual Standards. Critical Thinking. 2017.
http://www.criticalthinking.org/pages/universal-intellectual-standards/527

educational psychologist, author, teacher, presenter, President of the Foundation for Critical Thinking, and Executive Director of the Center for Critical Thinking.

In collaboration with other colleagues, Paul and Elder came up with a set of standards to apply to almost any situation called the "universal intellectual standards." The idea was that good reasoning must have nine characteristics; it must be clear, accurate, precise, relevant, logical, significant, fair, and have both breadth and depth. Like Wade and Tavris, Elder and Paul believed in the power of well-formulated inquiries to develop critical thinking; to uphold the universal standards and look at situations in more depth required the simple act of posing targeted questions. For example:

Clarity:
- Can you explain in more detail?
- Can you provide examples?

Accuracy:
- How could we verify that?
- Do any other sources support those findings?

Precision:
- Can you be more specific?
- Can you be more detailed in your description?

Relevance:
- How is that connected to the problem at hand?
- How does it help us solve the problem?

Depth:

- What makes this challenging?
- What are some difficulties we might have to overcome?

Breadth:

- Do we need to consider any other points of view?
- Are there any other ways we can look at this?

Logic:

- Does this information make sense with the other information we have?
- Does this go along with the evidence and fit into the bigger picture?

Significance:

- Is this the most important thing we should think about?
- Which idea is the most important for us to address?

Fairness:
- Have all perspectives been heard and represented?
- Are any of the facts being altered to support a certain opinion over others?
- Are all points of view being given equal attention?

Using these questions could help develop one's critical thinking skills into an automatic ability by creating natural paths in the brain that would encourage it to be more careful and thoughtful rather than relying on simple one-sided biases and stereotypes to fill in gaps in information and jump to solutions.

The Elements of Thinking

These universal intellectual standards could then be applied to what Paul and Elder deemed the "elements of thinking," or eight facets of reasoning that could be developed by frequently exploring lines of questioning like those above.

Purpose

Like taking a road trip without a map, thinking can get off track if it doesn't know where to go. All thinking has a goal, but knowing what that goal is will help set your sights and decide on your destination rather than wandering aimlessly and missing your objective completely. Whether you're trying to answer a question, solve a problem, or increase your knowledge, you have to know your purpose or else you won't know when you've gotten there. Along the way, you should also check in with yourself as a reminder of your purpose and affirm whether you're still going the right way or if you've veered off track.

Question

Just as Wade and Tavris highlighted the importance of asking questions with the right intent, Paul and Elder suggest that questions are necessary for focusing your thoughts. Not just any old question will do, however: it must be an inquiry that is worded and posed in a way that will facilitate your thinking and research. In the journey of critical thinking, your question is like your set of directions; they seem implicit, but they must be formulated in the right way to steer you correctly and often need to be broken down into smaller steps to guide you without becoming overwhelming.

Assumptions

Assumptions are a part of critical thinking that you don't choose to adopt, but which you must come to terms with, nevertheless.

Assumptions, similar to biases and stereotypes, are like the viewpoint from your vehicle. You can't help that they limit your perspective, yet you have to learn to navigate with them anyway. They're your blind spots, your distractions, and the lens through which you see the world. The view from a tinted window will be different from that of a clean, clear windshield. But it can be hard to grasp how the state of that window affects you, especially from within the car, because you've gotten so used to the way you see and deal with its issues subconsciously. Therefore, you must be careful, and always ask yourself whether your perspective is supported by evidence or feelings and beliefs.

Point of View

A passenger sees the world outside the car differently than the person in the backseat. If a person in the backseat sees a bird in the road and the passenger sees a flock, but the driver sees nothing, that doesn't mean that the former two were wrong. In thinking, you must also remember that everyone has their own seat from which to view the world and that the angles they have access to may allow them to see less (or more) than you do. That doesn't make what they see wrong, however, nor does it make it any less (or more) important; it is simply unlike your own. To get a full picture, equal weight should be given to all views no matter how contradictory these perspectives may be from the way you see things.

Information

Of course, in order to get an answer, research must be done and information must be gathered. Even if you have the directions to know where to go, the journey itself will bring a host of new levels of understanding and may even change your course completely depending on what obstacles or insights you stumble onto.

As you take in this information, you must ensure that it is accurate, relevant, and backed up by facts rather than being founded on feelings or opinions. Don't forget that, at this point of the process, assumptions, beliefs, and biases must also be taken into account no matter how subconscious they may be.

Throughout this undertaking, it's of the utmost importance to remain objective and keep an open mind. Let in information that disputes your own ideas and views although you may naturally wish to shut it down.

Inferences

When you pose a question, your mind anticipates that you want a solution and automatically tries to fulfill that request by producing conclusions with what information it has, creating inferences. But this can be like making up your own shortcuts without knowing where the road goes; they won't usually get you to the right place. Without enough information, the brain will fill in the gaps and rely on speculation too much for these conclusions to be accurate or reliable. So, wait to celebrate when you come up with an idea until you've checked whether it's based on evidence and makes logical sense.

Concepts

Concepts are crucial aspects of reasoning but must be used in the right way. Usually more vague than simple evidence and information, concepts are ideas and theories that start to emerge as you work through a problem, giving an overarching view of the journey's goals and discoveries. But these must also be looked at with some skepticism to make sure they can be justified. Allow your mind to remain open and be willing to explore alternative explanations to see if they fit. Don't rush the process along just to get to the destination.

Implications and Consequences

Implications and consequences are both results of reasoning, but the former is a product of thinking and the latter is a result of actions. However, both must be considered when using critical thinking. You can predict implications and consequences by asking: What does this conclusion mean for you or others? What happens if this course of action is followed through with? What happens if you do nothing? Be ready for where they may lead you and be aware that it might not always be a positive place.[17]

Valuable Intellectual Traits

Elder and Paul believed that the use of the universal intellectual standards in conjunction with the elements of reasoning would produce

---

[17] Elder, Linda. Paul, Richard. The Analysis & Assessment of Thinking. Critical Thinking. 2017.
http://www.criticalthinking.org/pages/the-analysis-amp-assessment-of-thinking/497

eight valuable intellectual traits in a person that would make them a great critical thinker.

Intellectual Humility

Humility is extremely beneficial to being a critical thinker but is difficult to achieve. You must go against your instinct to abide by your beliefs and not see your viewpoint as the best or only one. As humans, we're naturally proud, but we are also prone to making mistakes. Intellectually humble people are more willing to accept this and listen to others' ideas. Thus, they tend to be well-liked and respected because they make people feel heard and understood rather than just pushing their own convictions and trying to look or sound superior.[18]

---

[18] Westside Toastmasters. Intellectual Humility. Westside Toastmasters. 2018.
http://westsidetoastmasters.com/resources/thinking_tools/ch03lev1sec3.html

Intellectual Courage

It takes courage to be humble because it's difficult to put aside ideas you feel strongly about and step outside your own sphere of assumptions and biases into the unknown, especially when it may contrast or even disprove ideas you've held for so. But in order to find an answer that is right rather than one that just *feels* right or *seems* right, it's necessary to take into account as many sides as possible. If you don't look at something from all angles, it might be hiding something, like those art installations that appear to be a one-dimensional piece from the front but are really three-dimensional layers hanging from the ceiling and rising from the floor, creating different shapes depending on the angle you look at them. Only by stepping out of your comfort zone and exploring other avenues will you see the whole picture, but it takes bravery to walk that walk and risk your mind being altered forever.[19]

Intellectual Empathy

Remember that as much as you may want to prove yourself right, so does the person you're arguing with. No one wants to feel like a failure or to be proven wrong, and it's important to keep that in mind as you approach another person's stance. Others hold on to their beliefs just as strongly as you hold on to yours, even if those two things are complete opposites. Critical thinking is not about disproving another or proving yourself right, it's about getting to the correct answer … which might sometimes mean that no one is right.

---

[19] Westside Toastmasters. Intellectual Courage. Westside Toastmasters. 2018.
http://westsidetoastmasters.com/resources/thinking_tools/ch03lev1sec4.html

Intellectual Autonomy

You must accept responsibility for your thoughts. Don't accept opinions easily, but with careful and due diligence. Intellectual autonomy means avoiding following others just to fit in or being swayed to another's side. It's about standing up for yourself and making your own decisions based on proof, even if it means it sets you apart from everyone else. As Shakespeare once said, "This above all: to thine own self be true."[20] Even when it seems like you should go with what others are saying, if you always follow the evidence and keep your skepticism intact, you'll be more likely to be correct.[21]

---

[20] Literary Devices. To Thine Own Self Be True. Definition and Examples of Literary Terms. 2021. https://literarydevices.net/to-thine-own-self-be-true/

[21] Westside Toastmasters. Intellectual Autonomy. Westside Toastmasters. 2018. http://westsidetoastmasters.com/resources/thinking_tools/ch03lev1sec9.html

Intellectual Integrity

Intellectual integrity is holding yourself and everyone around you to high standards of basing arguments on proof rather than feelings or flimsy opinions. Integrity is also about being honest, to say you don't know something when you don't and to fess up when you've made a mistake, taking responsibility for that so you can make it right.[22] By doing this, you'll lead by example, asserting yourself as someone who is reliable, who knows what they're talking about, and who will encourage others to follow the path of evidence and reason. This will breed respect, and people will hold you in high esteem.

Intellectual Perseverance

---

[22] Westside Toastmasters. Intellectual Integrity. Westside Toastmasters. 2018.
http://westsidetoastmasters.com/resources/thinking_tools/ch03lev1sec6.html

There's no denying that critical thinking is a long road. Relying on biases and assumptions to make decisions and come to solutions would be a lot quicker and easier, but it wouldn't be right. The sacrifice for correctness and integrity is a waiting period. You'll have to be patient in order to get good answers and be able to wait it out and not rush to conclusions or solutions just for the purpose of having them. This won't be easy, especially when you face certain setbacks and challenges, but it will be worth it in the end to get not only an answer but greater understanding and knowledge.[23]

Confidence in Reason

To be patient, you must believe the end goal will be worth it. You must have confidence in

---

[23] Westside Toastmasters. Intellectual Perseverance. Westside Toastmasters. 2018.
http://westsidetoastmasters.com/resources/thinking_tools/ch03lev1sec7.html

the journey and that it will eventually bring you to honesty and truth. Although skepticism can be a useful trait, you can't just doubt everything you hear and see. You must also be able to rely on others and trust that they are reasonable, rational, critical thinkers (unless proven otherwise) who reason in ways that will benefit humanity.[24]

Fair-Mindedness

In being a critical thinker, you must not pass judgments or show favoritism. You must weigh all viewpoints equally and give everyone a fair chance to put forth their two cents on the matter. If you show prejudice or partiality towards any particular person or solution because of your own perspective, you tip the scales unfairly.[25]

---

[24] Westside Toastmasters. Confidence in Reason. Westside Toastmasters. 2018.
http://westsidetoastmasters.com/resources/thinking_tools/ch03lev1sec8.html

[25] Westside Toastmasters. What does fair mindedness requires? Westside Toastmasters. 2018. http://westsidetoastmasters.com/resources/thinking_tools/ch03lev1sec2.html

Chapter 4: Emotions, Assumptions, and Biases

There is a story from ancient times about Socrates standing at the gate of Athens with a young Plato when a young wayfarer walked by. As he walked past, the wayfarer asked Socrates, "Tell me, old man, how are the people of Athens? I heard that people here are quite unfriendly and treacherous."

"You are right," Socrates replied. "People you'll meet in Athens will be unfriendly and treacherous."

The stranger frowned, took a deep breath, and headed toward the city in a foul mood.

A few minutes later, another wayfarer arrived at the town gates and asked Socrates, "Tell me, old man, how are the people of Athens? I heard that people here are very welcoming and amicable."

"You are right," said Socrates. "People you'll meet in Athens will be welcoming and amicable."

As the second visitor entered the city with a smile on his face, the young Plato couldn't contain his curiosity. "Master, you told a lie to one of these people. You presented Athens in quite different ways."

"I didn't lie to either of them," said Socrates. "What they believe, they shall find."

Moods and Thinking

This story speaks to human nature and our tendency to accept what we assume and anticipate. More often than not, our mood is the deciding factor of how we approach or experience things. Our emotions are so powerful that they change our perspective about the information around us. Yet we may never even realize the extent of how much our thoughts affect our reality.

When someone asks us what we think about something, we often answer with how we feel rather than with logical statements. This is an unconscious and unintentional part of our intuition that recognizes an answer must be found quickly and reaches for the thing that's closest and easiest to grab. Feelings are quick solutions because they emerge readily and take no research or analysis to understand or formulate. But they are often wrong. We trick ourselves into accepting we've found a satisfying conclusion when, really, it has very little substance beyond what we believe and feel.

If we're stressed, our brains may assume we're in a survival situation that needs action where we need to be on high alert, and so tells us to be suspicious and stay focused. But if we're happy, we tell our brains that we're alright, allowing us to relax and be creative. Sometimes, however, we can put ourselves at too much ease, causing us to be less strict and more likely to make mistakes. The ideal is somewhere in between, where we can be quick to action but slow in thought … a difficult balance to achieve.

The Science Behind our Biases

Our desire for the world to make sense often wins out against our desire to be right. We piece together gaps in our knowledge by creating stories and beliefs so that we don't have to face the unknown. As humans, we are adept at underestimating our own ignorance. We don't know what we don't know, and we're usually okay with that, because if we did, we wouldn't be able to be as confident as we are.

Due to our "fight or flight" survival instincts, our brains want to make decisions as quickly as possible. Therefore, our minds are quick to jump to conclusions and make connections with stereotypes, biases, and assumptions. Thinking takes a lot of our energy and attention, which our brains don't like to use up if it's not absolutely necessary. Dr. Kahneman calls this way of thinking in shortcuts "fast thinking," which is in direct contrast to "slow thinking" or taking time to evaluate and set a course of action for a situation. Dr. Kahneman also refers to this "fast thinking" as System 1, or "the instant, unconscious, automatic, emotional, intuitive thinking," and "slow thinking" as System 2, or "the slower, conscious, rational, reasoning, deliberate thinking."[26] Where fast thinking is a gullible and quick-to-action young chap, slow thinking is like a ponderous old man full of wisdom.

Both types of thinking have their time and place and their pros and cons. "Fast thinking" allows you to check in with your worldview and baseline of normality, but it can be quick to believe things without evidence and isn't

---

[26] Kahneman, Daniel. Thinking Fast and Slow. Farrar, Straus and Giroux; 1st edition. 2013.

great at examining information. Meanwhile, "slow thinking" helps you slow down to ponder more deeply but will take its toll on your energy reserves and require much more time and effort.

Thinking slowly goes against human nature because it takes more time and effort than our brains want to give to problem-solving and acts against our survival instinct. It also asks us to question and be willing to disprove our own beliefs and accept the unfamiliar, things that our brains tell us are unnecessary risks that could get us into trouble. Because of how much energy it takes, we tend to only break out our slow thinking when we run into an unexpected problem or result. As things become too difficult, our brains come to accept that the problem can't be fixed so easily and finally give in to rolling up their sleeves and digging into the hard work.

In some ways, our brains are right in trying to make shortcuts. If we always thought about things in a slow, critical way, analyzing every piece of information and being skeptical of all that comes our way, it would be too exhausting for us. For some things, there's no need to break out the big critical-thinking guns, like for what you want to eat for lunch or what to wear to work. You *could* really break down these decisions and analyze them, but the result wouldn't be worth the effort.

However, many things in our lives *could* use a critical eye, such as: Whom to choose as a life partner and why? What's the best field of study or work we should pursue considering our abilities and interests? Who is a good advisor to us? Unfortunately, we just don't have enough effort and time to dedicate that level of thinking to everything. Therefore, part of critical thinking is knowing what to think critically about and what can be let go of. Sometimes, you'll have to settle for a middle ground. This compromise will allow you to reserve your energy for times that require all your critical processes. For example, slow thinking should be used when we're more apt to make mistakes, such as when we don't have much information on the subject and might jump to conclusions.

It's easiest to slip into fast thinking when we need it the least. Slow thinking is an invaluable skill, but one that doesn't come naturally, and must be built and exercised repeatedly to become more readily available. Slow thinking only really occurs in groups or businesses which tend to take a longer time to change or make decisions on things and have procedures in place to ensure alterations aren't made in haste.

To tame fast thinking, you can create your own procedure too. The first step is to take a breath to avoid making snap decisions. Then, you can use the methods of Elder and Paul or Wade and Tavris to work through your reasoning.

Jumping to Conclusions

When things occur too rapidly for our logical side to catch up with what's happening, we tend to jump to conclusions and take things as they are. Kahneman refers to this as a "what we see is all there is" mentality, assuming the existing information is *all* the information. Any gaps are filled in by judgments and speculation, leading to prejudice, inaccuracies, and misplaced trust.

In most cases, our brains do this so quickly that we don't notice, hiding the fact that it hasn't done its full calculations. But if we become more aware of what makes a good analysis and what common shortcuts are, we can become more cautious of them. There are a few common assumptions people often fall into that give the illusion of evidence but actually have little to back them up:

Law of Numbers

Just because a few people believe something or have something in common doesn't make it true, even if they are the loudest or have close connections to you. You must look at a greater population before taking into account people's opinions and experiences to know whether their results have been skewed by sample size to avoid making an overgeneralization about a larger group or trend.

Illusion of Understanding

"Happily ever after" is the type of ending we've become familiar with … perhaps to a fault. We like stories that wrap up nicely and neatly and are more willing to accept them. Even if it means cherry-picking what goes into that story so that the narrative makes sense, dismissing and conveniently forgetting things that go against the grain and ruin the overall arc.

Overly Optimistic

Being optimistic can be a good thing unless it goes too far. Becoming overly confident in good results can lead you to take unnecessary and ill-advised risks and lack preparation for possible failures and mistakes. Optimism must be realistic if it is to be successful, otherwise it will cloud your decision-making abilities.

Overconfidence

When we believe too strongly that we're right, we won't be able to accept we're wrong when we are. For example, Kahneman found that CFOs of large companies who were more resolute in their predictions of how S&P 500 companies would do in the next year had no greater chance of being right but were more confident in their companies. Thus, they were more willing to take greater risks with their business.[27] But these risks didn't always pan out the way their overly optimistic minds predicted.

---

[27] Kahneman, Daniel. Thinking Fast and Slow. Farrar, Straus and Giroux; 1st edition. 2013.

As humans, we're not very good at judging ourselves or our abilities. Thomas Gilovich, a psychologist at Cornell University, conducted a survey of one million high school seniors, asking them to rate their leadership skills. The results showed that 70% of participants thought themselves to be above average, with only 2% believing they were below average, an obvious statistical impossibility. Likewise, other studies have found that 94% of college professors believe they perform better than their colleagues, and most people identify themselves as above average in nearly every area of their life, from how lucky they are to how open-minded they can be. This overconfidence works the other way, too; the majority of people feel they are less likely than others to make mistakes ... which is obviously a mistake.[28]

Loss Aversion

Loss aversion is the opposite issue to overconfidence, but both lead to the same outcome: poor decision-making. Someone who is loss averse avoids risks to their detriment and the other takes far too many. Losses carry twice as much weight as gains and are much more memorable. Because of this, our brains become extra careful about things we've made mistakes on or failed at to avoid feeling that loss again, forcing us to make certain decisions that might be too

---

[28] Dunning, D., Meyerowitz, J., & Holzberg, A. Ambiguity and Self-Evaluation: The Role of Idiosyncratic Trait Definitions in Self-Serving Assessments of Ability. In T. Gilovich, D. Griffin, & D. Kahneman (Eds.), Heuristics and Biases: The Psychology of Intuitive Judgment (pp. 324-333). Cambridge: Cambridge University Press. doi:10.1017/CBO9780511808098.020. 2002. https://www.cambridge.org/core/books/heuristics-and-biases/ambiguity-and-selfevaluation-the-role-of-idiosyncratic-trait-definitions-in-selfserving-assessments-of-ability/AD02843FDFE75A167603DA6469565562

careful or too hazardous, or simply too based on our emotional response rather than our logical reasoning.

Types of Biases

Our biases often stem from a subconscious fear, whether that's fear of change, fear of being wrong, fear of no longer fitting in, fear of giving up something we've become used to, or fear of being seen as unintelligent. We often stick by our beliefs not only because they help us feel as if we're right, but because we don't want to give up their company or be ousted for having a different position than those we like to keep company with. Or we may stick by our arguments after standing by them for so long because it is easier than apologizing and feeling the discomfort of admitting we were wrong.

Yet, our biases are just one of many hurdles standing in the way of critical thinking, alongside peer pressure, blaming others, being defensive, resistance to change, ignorance, pride, close-mindedness, greed, denial, apathy, superstition, and poor communication skills.

All these barriers preventing us from reaching our full potential have one thing in common: They take us out of control of the outcome. That way, we no longer have to be to blame for our actions. But it isn't worth it. When we hand our decision-making over to our assumptions, they follow their own course that puts little emphasis on our wants and desires. All we can do is buckle up and hold on as they take the wheel and drive us to our snap decision, a short yet perilous journey with many bumps in the road. But critical thinking can teach us to predict outcomes more accurately, guiding us to more informed conclusions.

By educating yourself about forms of common biases, you can start to see how they emerge in other people's attitudes and marketing, but also yourself. This awareness can help you establish tools for minimizing your reliance on them, allowing you to be less partial and more open-minded, making you a better critical thinker.

Belief Bias

Belief bias follows syllogistic reasoning, or relying too much on prior premises, rather than fully formed ideas of concepts. This can be most easily demonstrated with syllogisms, which ask for a conclusion to be drawn from a particular set of statements using speculation. Similarly to analogies, syllogisms seek to draw connections between two concepts but can too often lead to ambiguity and mistaken reasoning. Syllogisms are frequently used to test on their deductive reasoning but is not a great method for real-life analysis as they can produce incorrect conclusions.

Take a moment to look at a few syllogisms and think about whether the conclusions are believable or not:

Most birds fly. An ostrich is a bird. Therefore, an ostrich flies.

This syllogism may make sense, but the use of "most" gives away the fact that it is invalid. Although this first sentence is correct, it is vague and leaves out information necessary for the conclusion. If "most" birds fly, there are some that don't, but it gives us no insight into what those might be. And it just so happens that one such type is ostriches.

All fish have gills. An octopus has gills. Therefore, an octopus is a fish.

Again, this statement creates an overgeneralization that leaves out pertinent information. Although all fish indeed have gills, not all animals with gills are fish. An octopus may have gills, but it is a mollusk.

Colorful snakes are venomous. A king snake is colorful. Therefore, a king snake is venomous.

This one is the trickiest of the three. The first statement says that colorful snakes are venomous, but not that *all* colorful snakes are. You might assume it means all snakes, but it is not explicitly stated. Indeed, bright and colorful snakes are often venomous, but not all of them. Because we don't know what colorful snakes we are referring to or, for that matter, what type of king snake, we don't have enough information to decide whether the statement is true. Although the final sentence is factual, it is not clear enough to be successful or true.

Syllogisms may not be very useful for coming to conclusions, but they are very efficient for exploring people's acceptance of assumptions, such as in the study conducted by Jonathan Evans, Julie Barston, and Paul Pollard. By using syllogisms to look at belief bias, the three found that reasoning and questioning were only used in figuring out problems when the conclusions were found to be unbelievable.[29] This finding proves our brains only used that extra effort when it was unavoidable.

---

[29] St. B. T. Evans, Jonathan & L. Barston, Julie & Pollard, Paul. On the Conflict between Logic and Belief in Syllogistic Reasoning. Memory & cognition. 11. 295-306. 10.3758/BF03196976. 1983.
https://www.researchgate.net/publication/16575665_On_the_Conflict_between_Logic_and_Belief_in_Syllogistic_Reasoning

Confirmation Bias

We like being right. And we like when people agree with us. Therefore, we more readily accept those ideas that are in alignment with our own. We are attracted to information that furthers or supports our ideas and have a natural distaste for anything that goes against them. This disposition makes us more argumentative or causes us to disbelieve information we don't like, as we're less willing to be proven wrong than to be proven right. This relates back to our overconfident nature, which makes us feel as if we *must* be right and persuades us against any inkling we may be wrong.[30] With this type of thinking, we tend to stick with what we're familiar with

---

[30] Shea, Brendan. Karl Popper: Philosophy of Science. Internet Encyclopedia of Philosophy. 2018.
https://www.iep.utm.edu/pop-sci/

and ignore important evidence we don't want to see.

For example, if you're friends with someone, you'll be more willing to stand up for them and argue their strengths and achievements when someone doubts their abilities. Similarly, if a person believes that a border collie is the best type of dog to have as a pet, they will always choose to adopt border collies and never try another breed. Any facts about border collies being superior will be noted while those in favor of other species will not.

Hindsight Bias

Hindsight is 20/20. And because we want to be right about things, we often take on this new, guaranteed-right perspective and pretend we were in the know about it all along. This puts emphasis on the end result of a situation rather than the process of getting there and leads to laying blame or credit on outside sources rather than becoming better at predicting results.

For example, a person may watch a lottery drawing and, upon seeing a certain number come up, express that they were going to buy a ticket. They would suggest they would have won had they just stopped at the store and blame their failure to do so on other situations or people in their life that forced them to come home quickly.

Egocentric Bias

Because we tend to be such an overconfident species, we often overestimate what we can do. This can cause us to argue with authorities because we think we know more than other people and believe so strongly in our own judgments that we accept no other. We may also end up attacking a person rather than their argument in order to try to "win" and make them feel inferior. For example, saying something is "stupid" rather than saying their "arguments are unintelligent."

Egocentrism often comes in the form of phrases and thoughts such as:

- "It's true because I believe it."
- "It's true because we believe it." (Sociocentrism)
- "It's true because I want to believe it."
- "It's true because I have always believed it."
- "It's true because it is in my personal interest to believe it."[31]

---

[31] O'Reilly, Kim. PhD. Why Critical Thinking Is So Important. Intercultural Solutions. 2008.
https://www.interculturalsolutions.net/why-critical-thinking-

Marketing and Manipulation

Our biases aren't just something we use as a crutch, but something others use to manipulate us. Often, these people may not even realize how much they may be influencing us, and neither will we unless we watch out for it. The same goes for us controlling others. However, there is one place where the manipulators are well aware of how they use our assumptions against us.

Manipulation is most commonly found in marketing. When you pay attention to your daily media intake, you'll find yourself surrounded by these inundating messages. A large chunk of an hour-long television show is

is-so-important/

peppered with commercials. Also, much of the social media we scroll past in our daily lives is sponsored or put out by advertisers.
Everywhere you turn, messages in the media are trying to persuade you to believe, buy, or do something.

These messages have a language all their own. They have such a limited amount of time to grab your attention and communicate with you that every single word is chosen with deliberate care. They do not select neutral or random words; nothing is left to chance when it comes to how they want you to receive and interpret their messages.

Advertisers' number-one goal is to persuade you to buy their product or service, but that doesn't just go for a cute pair of shoes or a writing course. Public relations experts will also try to "sell" you an image, such as a positive impression of a candidate, company, or organization. Campaigning or advocacy groups may also try to persuade you to buy into certain beliefs, values, issues, or policies. Advertising for specific candidates attempt to convince you that the opinions they present are factual in order to get you to believe what they say in debates and elect them to political office or to pass their amendment.[32]

No matter what the goal is, marketers all use specific language to persuade us, usually by connecting to their target audience with something they're known to already favor and like. For example, they might use a well-loved celebrity who people trust to be the "face" of their product. Or they may use ads that use

---

[32] New Mexico Media Literacy Project. The Language of Persuasion. New Mexico Media Literacy Project. 2007. https://www.greenwichschools.org/uploaded/faculty/maryellen_brezovsky/CMS/8_Media_Literacy/The_Language_of_Persuasion.pdf

appealing imagery like smiling people or cute animals.

For example, Tom Selleck and the late Alex Trebek are popular celebrity figures, especially to those in older generations. Therefore, advertisers use them to inspire trust in services such as reverse home mortgages and life insurance policies which are targeted at a similar audience. Nike, on the other hand, usually tries to target younger generations and does so by bringing in popular athletes who appeal to these age groups for their advertising campaigns like Colin Kaepernick and LeBron James.

When it comes to creating a positive image for a candidate running for office, you will probably see commercials depicting them as being involved in their community or as very committed and close to their families, showing imagery that would suggest they're relatable and trustworthy. Or you might see those campaign and advocacy groups that seek to create a negative image of an opponent and try to evoke a feeling of anger or fear in the people who see their advertisements to bring them to their side. This occurs most notably with political ads, which usually show a candidate in stark black and white with ominous music playing over unflattering and fear-inducing pictures and text. If the goal is to persuade people that a candidate doesn't care about the environment, for example, the ad will show images of factories polluting the air, water filled with sludge or oil, and sick animals. This type of ad aims to associate a candidate or political issue with something that they believe their target voters don't like, creating a strong emotional response that will leave a lasting impression people will remember when it comes time to vote.

The horror stories depicted in ads are often exaggerated, irrelevant to people's lives, or use selectively chosen information or even skewed facts and figures. Still, they successfully generate a strong and lasting emotional transfer in their target audience through their use of implied association.

Those who are savvy in marketing know their target audience well and are adept at tailoring their message in such a way that it will be extremely persuasive to them, sometimes imperceptibly. We are exposed to this multiple times a day without even realizing it's happening. But we can educate ourselves about their common strategies to be more aware of how we're being manipulated.

Going Along with the Crowd

This trick plays on our human tendency to want to fit in with the group. Psychology calls this cognitive bias the "bandwagon effect."

This technique depicts a product or service making large groups of people happy or improving their lives to suggest that "everyone is doing it" and causing those who aren't to feel left out. For example, if an ad were to say that a high percentage of people use a certain supplement for sleep, we'll be led to believe that most people are using it and might want to try it ourselves. This can be even more compelling when those using it are celebrities we trust or even one our friends and neighbors recommended.

Live Up to a High Standard of Success

This tactic capitalizes on our desire to be like our role models or people we look up to. Marketers use celebrities, attractive people, and those who are seen as wealthy or successful because they know we want to achieve things we assume these famous people already have. By portraying our idols using their products, advertisers create an impression that the celebrity's beauty or achievements are in some ways connected to the item they're selling. This makes us feel as if similar success is within our reach if we only use what's being sold to us.

"Trust Me, I'm an Expert."
It's in our nature as humans to put high value on the sentiments of people we see as experts. Therefore, many people in commercials are dressed as doctors, scientists, teachers, and other professionals who are taken in our society to be trustworthy. Logically, we may comprehend they're only actors, but the imagery of them as an expert in the area they're speaking about can be a powerful, persuasive tool.

Flattery

In the words of Mae West, "Flattery will get you everywhere."[33] Marketers know that everyone likes to be complimented, so they go out of their way to make their target audience feel special and as if they value their opinions, purchasing decisions, and judgment.

That Loving Feeling

Marketing experts also like to include images of things people love, enjoy, and find comforting because they create positive feelings in the people they want to sell to. Thus, people become connected with their product or brand. This might be anything from cute animals to loving families celebrating the holidays together, or curling up by the fire with a warm blanket and a book to strolling

---

[33] Quotemaster. Flattery will get you everywhere. - Mae West. Quotemaster. 2021.
https://www.quotemaster.org/q825fde4a9be73cd0d44d44bbe05a2c8d

along the beach at sunset. The hope is to associate a sense of happiness with their candidate, product, service, or message.

Scientific Evidence

This may appear to be a trustworthy tactic, but it can be manipulated. This is a particular approach where marketers strengthen their message with science. They use charts, graphs, and statistics that the average Joe doesn't understand to prove their product is legit or skew the data so they look and sound more impressive than they are. This is persuasive because many people trust science and numbers to provide logical proof.

Simple Solution

Our life is so complicated, we are so complex, our problems are so hard to solve … But XYZ company has a unique, simple solution to all of these issues. Isn't that nice to hear? Of course it is! Marketers know this and often offer help by proposing a "simple," "quick," or "easy" solution. Advertisers take this strategy as far as suggesting that a car, a brand, or a cleaning product will make you desirable, popular, a good mom, successful, wealthy, and so on.[34]

Chances are you're familiar at least one of these strategies. But did you see it at the time for what it was? Don't feel bad if you didn't. Marketers are good at their jobs: manipulating us in order to sell products. And they're purposefully sneaky about it. If you knew you were being manipulated, after all, you wouldn't allow for it. Meanwhile, we're so

---

[34] New Mexico Media Literacy Project. The Language of Persuasion. New Mexico Media Literacy Project. 2007. https://www.greenwichschools.org/uploaded/faculty/maryellen_brezovsky/CMS/8_Media_Literacy/The_Language_of_Persuasion.pdf

inundated with these types of messages every day that it's hard to escape their pull toward biased information.

Being sold on a product isn't always a bad thing, but knowing the types of strategies that are used to get you to think, vote, or buy a certain way will help you see what thoughts are your own and what thoughts have been put into your mind by imagery, assumptions, and advertising. The trick is to be able to be aware of biases and trapping techniques and to separate this information from cold, hard data.

How to Detect Biases in Data and Information

What's the difference between data and information? Data is just facts, while information is what we do with those facts in order to draw conclusions. How do we sort that information? How do we present it? And who do we present it to? These are all crucial steps of the process but ones that can quickly succumb to the hazards of implicit bias.

Suppose I want to increase my savings. I sit down and create a budget and see how much I can put away every month. I download an app that rounds up and saves extra change when I use my debit card and set up an automatic transfer to put aside 10% of my paycheck every week. Then, I track my progress and see my account grow. Over time, I can graph what that growth looks like and even predict when I'll meet my goals. I can see how long it will take to earn X amount of money and compare those numbers to what I had hypothesized to see the difference. That's data.

But if I start using that data to plan a trip or use it to look at when I could retire, it becomes information. It's no longer about the numbers but what they mean in a real-life application. The problem is that when we begin to interpret data and turn it into information, we always run the risk of making mistakes and allowing our biases to get in the way of our objectivity.

For example, if I had a negative outlook on money and assumed the worst, I may have a hard time looking positively at the data for my savings. The numbers would be the same as if I had a positive outlook, but because of my strong feelings on the matter, I can't help but project negativity onto the data, altering it in my eyes. I see that I can retire at a certain age based on my calculations but believe due to past experiences that I will never be able to or that I won't have enough. This feeling isn't based on anything scientific or factual but is hard to resist, nonetheless.

Data can just as easily be skewed by our prejudices before it has been concluded. For example, if I tracked my savings but didn't factor in my expenses, it would be an incomplete picture of my total finances and wouldn't allow me to draw accurate interpretations. If we don't catch these types of mistakes, we'll end up following through and coming to verdicts that can't be relied on. I may determine that I can retire even earlier than I expected. It would be based on facts and would add up mathematically. But if I had not factored in my expenses, I would eventually find that this number would not be accurate.

Unfortunately, there is no way to completely escape or eradicate our biases. They're annoying, but they make us human. We can, however, work to minimize them with our critical-thinking skills.

Kahneman comes up with several questions we should ask when we're presented with information to identify whether biases exist, including when we present them to ourselves:

- What might be the biases of the people presenting an idea or recommendation? Some of the most common are that they might be overconfident, have a strong connection to past experiences, or be concerned with their own self-interest and well-being.

- Are those making a recommendation passionate about what they recommend? Chances are high they are, otherwise, they wouldn't recommend it. But this favoritism for the product or service can skew their perspective.

- Did people reach a conclusion just because that's what the others in the group decided and they wanted to fit in and go along with the group? Or were dissenting opinions also discussed and considered?[35]

Kahneman believes that decision-making should not be left up to chance ... or even to your own devices. Your best odds are to assemble a team of people who are willing and able to challenge each other to take in differing viewpoints. Whether at work, in life, or both, surrounding yourself with "yes men" will do you no favors. Instead, try to bring together those who won't be afraid to stand up and speak their mind, especially those who have different experiences than yourself. Having these people on your side will be the greatest way to bring awareness to your biases and keep them in check.

---

[35] Kahneman, Daniel. Thinking Fast and Slow. Farrar, Straus and Giroux; 1st edition. 2013.

Minimize the Impact of Your Biases

It's almost impossible to completely eliminate biases, but you can minimize their impact. The first step is to get to know what your cognitive biases are and when they become a part of your thinking. Come to terms with the effect they have on your life, your outlook, and your decision-making abilities.

Then, you need to work hard to combat the natural instincts your predilections produce by reminding yourself often of why you hold those beliefs and what evidence backs them up. This will be a constant and ongoing process that must be revisited every time you make a decision. Biases are tricky things and, if you turn your back, can sneak back up on you and make themselves at home without you even realizing it.

Self-awareness or metacognition is your greatest tool against letting your leanings hold you back. Easier said than done, but it will be worth it to more deeply understand how your mind operates and will allow you to process and comprehend information more efficiently.

The next best strategy is to ensure that you're careful to take an evidence-first approach. You can help yourself do this by partaking in habits like keeping a journal so you can have a record of events as they happened rather than relying on your memory, creating psychological distance by removing yourself from judgments and ignoring how others may be feeling about you, and by being open to other outcomes and opinions even if they go against your own.[36]

---

[36] Soll, Jack B. Milkman, Katherine L., Payne, John W. A User's Guide To Debiasing. 2018.
http://www.opim.wharton.upenn.edu/~kmilkman/Soll_et_al_2013.pdf

Reflection: Are You Ready to Take on Your Biases?

Take a moment to ask yourself the following questions, being honest with yourself. Really mull them over rather than providing a fast-thinking, gut-response answer.

- Why is it beneficial to develop critical-thinking skills? Are they necessary?
- What rewards and challenges can you expect?
- Are you willing to put in the necessary time and effort? Is it something you're ready to commit to?
- Are you ready to start combating the barriers to critical thinking so that you can overcome them?
- Do you realize that this is a lifelong process and that you will always be a

work in progress, constantly trying to improve your skills?

- What steps do you need to take to begin developing your critical-thinking skills?
- Will you be able to communicate with people who aren't critical thinkers, and whose barriers prevent them from participating in a respectful and meaningful discussion? Or should you not even try to communicate with them?
- How should you react when a lack of critical-thinking skills is evident in your friends and family, colleagues, the media, or other settings?

Now take a look at my bias detection worksheet. Whenever you are about to make an important (or not so important) decision and you have a choice in mind, double-check your hidden motivations. Use it as a practicing tool to explore, assess, and yourself with your biases:

Question/Bias	Bias 1	Bias 2	Bias 3	Bias 4
Why do I lean toward saying yes/no? What knowledge/ resource do I base my choice on?				
Where does my source get their information? Is their source science-based or anecdote-based?				
What emotions guided me when				

I made up my mind about my decision? Did I feel this emotion before when making a decision? What was the outcome of that decision?				
What bias—if any—can I identify based on my decision-making process?				
Have I listened to the same information source before? Did their advice bring me closer				

to my goals? If yes, why? If no, why?				
Do my decisions in general improve my life? If yes, what am I doing well? If not, what am I doing wrong?				
What could I do differently next time to improve my decision-making?				

We all carry our bias baggage with us wherever we go. Our preconceived ideas are a part of us we must accept. But if we're going to come to a deeper understanding of things in life, we'll have to acknowledge the baggage we carry and be willing to check it at the gate when it's too heavy for us to bring aboard a discussion or debate. Only then will we be unburdened enough for us to fly and learn new ideas.

Overcoming biases is difficult, but it is worthwhile. It will allow you to have a more open mind, meet new people, and improve your relationships. Without them holding you back, you'll be able to achieve your personal and professional goals, make informed decisions, and experience a greater sense of purpose and satisfaction.

Chapter 5: How to Understand More Deeply

Edward Burger and Michael Starbird, authors of *The Five Elements of Effective Thinking*, believe that "any subject or concept (no matter how complex they are) is just a combination of a few simple core ideas. The fundamentals always govern concepts all around us."[37]

This may seem overgeneralized, but think about it. Anything you learn comes down to just a few basics that made up your early education. Whether it was learning your sight words and multiplication tables or how to ride

---

[37] Burger, E. B., & Starbird, M. P. (2012). The 5 elements of effective thinking. Princeton University Press.

a bike as a child, it opened up a whole new world. Suddenly, reading and math weren't so difficult and didn't take so long to work through. Riding a bike became as easy as … well, riding a bike, and created a whole new sense of freedom and mobility. But it all comes back to those core concepts which laid the foundation that enabled you to do more and more wonderful and challenging things as you continued to learn and grow.

Once you've mastered the fundamentals, you'll find yourself leaning on those core concepts as you're presented with more difficult stages. This is true no matter the skill—whether you're learning to drive or cook or studying quantum physics. These skills will never leave you; they'll continue to be there to help you build and expand on your knowledge and abilities.

In a way, this is like leveling up in a video game. The tutorial you have in the beginning may be simplistic, but it teaches you what buttons to push. Without that lesson, the rest of the game would be impossible. Those buttons are the core of everything you do in the game and will never change. The game doesn't get harder by adding more buttons, it merely asks you to use them in new ways. Mastering the combos is a matter of putting those button presses together in the right order and with the right timing. At each level, you'll be asked to get a little bit more out of those series of presses and clicks, building off what you did in the previous round until you get better and better. And eventually, those same buttons will bring you to victory! At that point, the simple "press A to kick" is second nature, a small part of overall mastery and competency.

When you start to look at your abilities in these terms, advanced study becomes a lot more manageable and less intimidating, giving you more confidence to take on challenges. You'll know what you need to succeed—you just have to put the pieces together in the right way.

Similarly, the key to approaching a complex concept is to break it down into more manageable parts and steps. Work on the simpler concepts and then move ahead to the more difficult aspects in order to gain a deeper understanding. This begins with figuring out what's really important.

Home in on what the point of it all is, the heart of the matter, and put the other bits aside that could distract you so you can focus on just the core pieces of the problem. Master the basics and don't allow the rest to overwhelm you. After you become familiar with these fundamentals, then you can bring the other stuff back in.

That doesn't mean you should just go and ignore the extras. If you do, you won't get a full appreciation. But compartmentalizing things so you can take them on one at a time is much more manageable. This is like drawing; if you don't sketch out the shape of what you want to make an image of first, there's no use in adding in color and details. You have to start with the basic shapes and work your way up. By doing this, you allow yourself to use your energy and attention on the heart of the problem when it's at its height, making you more productive. This method also allows you to see how the parts and pieces are connected and leaves more room for you to be creative. Breaking it up into steps also helps to make it feel like you're making greater progress, giving you more to check off your to-do list and allowing you to become more confident as you work away at it bit by bit.

Starbird and Burger ascribe to the idea that brilliant thinkers are not born but made and developed through years of practice. They came up with specific core strategies that can be used to ameliorate our thinking skills. These techniques are ones we use in our daily lives without realizing how much they can impact us. But if we knew how to properly develop and build off them so they can be used in more complex ways, we would unlock a world of deeper understanding. In essence, these elements could be broken down into three simple concepts: make mistakes, ask questions, and allow yourself to think deeply.

Make Mistakes and Ask Questions

Many people fear making mistakes because they assume it reflects badly upon them. But mistakes are really just learning opportunities in disguise. When we make mistakes, we can use them for self-improvement. We just have to take the time to analyze what went wrong instead of trying to cover them up or forget about them. Errors are merely a natural source of feedback, a way for us to find out where our perception is lacking and fill in the gaps. But they don't just point out what we're doing wrong, they can also show us what we're doing right. When properly dissected, failure can even be just as beneficial to helping us figure out the solution to a problem as doing something correctly.

Michael Jordan is a great example of someone who interpreted this well. He could have easily looked at being cut from his high school basketball team as defeat and given up, but he didn't. He chose to learn from the experience and work even harder. He went on to win six championships and five MVPs in his career and is seen as one of the greatest basketball players of all time. He once said, "I have missed more than 9,000 shots in my career. I have lost almost 300 games. On twenty-six occasions, I have been entrusted to take the game-winning shot, and I missed. I have failed over and over and over again in my life. And that is why I succeed."[38]

In reality, research is all about making mistakes. You can't know whether something is true or will work unless it's tested. And, when something is tested for the first time, it will often fail. But when we make a hypothesis in science, and it ends up wrong,

---

[38] Walter, Ekaterina. Fail Your Way To Amazing Things. Forbes. 2013.
https://www.forbes.com/sites/ekaterinawalter/2013/10/29/fail-your-way-to-amazing-things/#c92e41167596

we don't see that as a waste of time. That research is still highly viable and valuable because it has proven something is *not* the case.

We must test things. Try as we might to envision every possible outcome and consequence of our ideas, we will always miss some unless we put them into action. We can't let our fear of failing prevent us from making progress.

In *The Five Elements of Effective Thinking*, Burger and Starbird stress the importance of learning from your mistakes by asking:

- What went wrong?
- What can you learn from your mistakes?
- What can you do differently in the future?[39]

---

[39] Burger, E. B., & Starbird, M. P. (2012). The 5 elements of

In contrast, Burger and Starbird also suggest you must analyze what you're doing that *is* working by asking:

- Why did this work?
- How can it be repeated in the future?
- What went right?

To learn from our mistakes, we must ask ourselves questions to assess and analyze. But questions are not just there to help us learn from our failure and success, but to help us learn about almost everything … if we pose them correctly.

Ask Questions

Asking questions is something people tend to avoid for fear that it will expose them to ridicule by revealing what they don't know. But no one can know everything. Asking questions is the best way to learn and develop

---

effective thinking. Princeton University Press.

and is much better than remaining ignorant about something.

There is a saying that "if you only do what you've always done, then you will always get what you always got." While there is some debate on where this quote comes from, the wisdom of the words definitely applies to our quest for greater understanding. Humans are creatures of habit. If something has been done before in a way that proved successful, it is seen as surefire. Why risk a new take or idea when it could lead to failure? "If it ain't broke, don't fix it," as they say. But such an approach causes stagnation. If we never seek to grow and learn (accepting that mistakes may occur), change will never happen in ourselves or the world. We are all works in progress, and so are our ideas and theories. There is always room for growth.

To make changes and access a current system or set of information, the first step is to question. Just as Tarvis and Wade and Elder and Paul highlighted the importance of questioning in critical thinking, Burger and Starbird emphasize the skill as one of the core aspects of developing our minds. Likewise, they assert that assumptions should be challenged, whether they belong to us or others. In this case, challenging doesn't mean disproving or becoming hostile but simply having what Wade and Tarvis would call a healthy dose of skepticism and curiosity. Asking questions doesn't mean you're unintelligent—it simply shows your willingness to learn new things.

If people never asked questions, we would know very little. If Newton never questioned the falling of an apple from a tree, we may have never had the theory of gravity. If we had never questioned whether we could go into space, we never would have traveled to the moon. And had we never questioned what came before us, we may never have discovered extinct species like dinosaurs and came to the theory of evolution.

You see, only questions can lead to answers.

Many philosophers and great people of history are known for the discoveries they made from questions, especially Socrates, who was naturally apt at raising questions and even developed a process based on it called the Socratic method. Yet, Socrates never thought of himself as having great wisdom—all he knew was that he sought it throughout his life: "One thing only I know, and that is that I know nothing."[40] He was always asking

---

[40] Goodreads. Socrates. Goodreads. 2021.
https://www.goodreads.com/quotes/738227-one-thing-only-i-know-and-that-is-that-i

questions, far more than he answered. And he learned a lot because of it.

Questions are the key to thinking critically, allowing us to gain a deeper understanding of ourselves and the world around us. However, it's vital to not only examine new ideas and information but to also frequently evaluate older beliefs and convictions we already hold dear to make certain they're based on facts and evidence rather than feelings and biases.

Asking Questions in Different Situations

Questions are a huge part of critical thinking and are emphasized by both Elder and Paul and Tarvis and Wade. But, as we've discussed, asking questions isn't a simple task. It's an art.

Without the right inquiry, we won't have the proper direction for our thoughts and can become lost. We may even find the wrong answer. Thus, depending on what we're looking for, our question should be worded differently to focus on the type of result we're looking for.[41]

If your goal is to remember, for example, you'll want to ask questions that will have answers that lend themselves well to memory, such as systems that involve lists or that focus on identifying, describing, or naming things, like:

- What do we already know about this topic?
- How does what we're learning now fit in with what we learned earlier on?

---

[41] Westside Toastmasters. What does fair mindedness requires? Westside Toastmasters. 2018.
http://westsidetoastmasters.com/resources/thinking_tools/ch03lev1sec2.html

To understand something, you'll want to prompt yourself to interpret the deeper meaning by describing, explaining, or predicting an outcome, such as by asking:

- What does this mean?
- What might the result be if this or that happened?
- Can you summarize the core ideas?

If you want to apply information you've learned to a new situation, you'll want to prompt yourself to demonstrate, hypothesize, solve, or implement by asking questions such as:

- What would happen if this changed?
- How could this be used in a different or new way?
- What is an additional example?

If you wish to analyze information, you'll want to break it down into smaller pieces for closer study by looking to compare and contrast, organize, and sort. You can do this by asking questions such as:

- How is this piece of information different than others?
- Why is this fact or evidence important?
- How are these pieces of information alike? Can you explain how or why?

To evaluate information for its significance based on certain standards, you'll look to judge, critique, conclude about, assess, or explain with questions such as:

- Do you agree or disagree with the information? What evidence do you have to support your answer?
- Why is this happening?

- How does this affect other things?

You can also formulate questions about constructing, planning, and creating to prompt new levels of thinking. Find new ways of looking at things by asking:

- What do you think causes this?
- What is another way of looking at this?
- What is a possible solution to this problem?

These are by no means the only questions to use. But they can act as a guide to help you begin to see the impact of how the wording of a question can affect the outcome and shape your thinking. To make sure you board a good train of thought, however, you'll need to know what direction you're trying to go and think about what will get you there. Grasping the goal of the question you need to ask is something you'll pick up over time by becoming more familiar with how people learn and how our brains function.

Follow the Flow of Ideas and Embrace Change

Burger and Starbird reasoned that "everything great that has ever happened to humanity has begun with an idea in someone's mind. So, in order to create something, you need a constant flow of ideas. Everything, whether it's a physical product, a concept, or an idea came from someplace, it has arrived where it is now and is going to change in the future. It's a constant evolution."[42]

Only one thing in life is certain: It is constantly changing.

---

[42] Burger, Edward B. Starbird, Michael. Five Elements Of Effective Thinking. Princeton University Press. 2012.

Burger and Starbird identify the final element of effective thinking as change, citing that knowledge in any field doubles every five years. This means that not only is new knowledge increasing at an incredibly rapid rate, but that current information is just as quickly becoming obsolete.[43]

It's like being on a treadmill that never stops moving; if you don't keep pace with it, you'll fall off. To keep up, you must accept that change is inevitable and embrace it. When you're ready for change, you'll be more willing and able to adapt to it. If you let yourself follow the flow of ideas and information as they evolve, the tides will naturally bring you up to speed.

Part of this worldview is accepting that there is never an end. That's the beauty of learning:

---

[43] Burger, Edward B. Starbird, Michael. Five Elements Of Effective Thinking. Princeton University Press. 2012.

that it's limitless. Conclusions may seem and feel final, but they are only a step in a process of ever-changing and growing ideas, a piece of a puzzle that has no borders and can shift and grow at all times. Discoveries are merely successes in a series of more discoveries. Much like a pebble tossed in the water, the ripples from a new idea extend in all directions. Where its influence stops, no one can be sure.

Being a critical thinker is about being a student of the world. It's about overcoming our naturally occurring overconfidence and adopting a humble attitude. There is too much information out there for us to know it all or to always be right. So, we have two options: shut it out and pretend we're always correct while knowing deep down that it's not true, or open our mind to learning and risk being wrong. The former will allow you to avoid fessing up to mistakes, but the latter will allow you to evolve and grow as a person. If we don't continue to learn, we'll become stagnant and never grow or evolve.

There's always more to be learned. But, in order to learn it, you must be open to following ideas and never settling for the limits of your current knowledge, because there is always more out there. Discoveries will naturally occur if you are willing to accept new insights and evidence and seek to build off what those who came before you have contributed. Question and confirm their findings and then expand them to create new ideas of your own. As Thomas Edison once said, "I start where the last man left off … Many of life's failures are people who didn't realize how close they were to success when they gave up."[44]

---

[44] Brainy Quote. Thomas A. Edison. Brainy Quote. 2021.

When we know better, we do better. When we think critically, we gain better information. When we have better information, we can make better decisions. Taking in facts from a variety of sources and analyzing them leads to a deeper understanding. And being able to connect the ideas from various disciplines and sources makes discoveries much more likely. But all this starts with simply learning anything and everything you can.

---

https://www.brainyquote.com/quotes/thomas_a_edison_109004

Chapter 6: Reasoning by Analogy

Hammer is to nail as ___ is to hair. Chances are you've answered your fair share of analogy questions like this on tests throughout your academic career, especially if you went to school in the U.S. But have you ever wondered why? Research has found that the part of our brains we use to work out analogies may also be a core part of our creativity. This means that the ability to make and comprehend these connections might not just be academically beneficial but can be used in our reasoning to come to new conclusions no one has yet tried.

Analogies compare two unlike things to highlight a connection that may not be obvious, leading us to consider how dissimilar things have similarities. By strengthening this muscle in our mind, we can start to see how things are associated in our reasoning and lead us to better understand how concepts relate. Both skills are core concepts of critical thinking, which is why analogies are so often used when looking to test or improve our reasoning abilities.

On the surface, analogies may all seem the same, but depending on the wording and items chosen, they can flex quite separate parts of our brain. For example, the analogy "A piano is to keyboard as a drum is to ___" has the solution of "percussion." This type of analogy is most concerned with measuring a person's capability to categorize objects and is often found on simple logic tests.

Often in analogy tests the purpose is to gauge how well the subject can draw connections between words and definitions. For example, the analogy "Cultivate is to nurture as expectation is to ___." This requires more creativity than the previous analogy as there are multiple correct answers. Cultivate and nurture are synonyms, so we know that the answer will be a synonym to "expectation." This could be "hope," "belief," "assumption," or a handful of other possibilities. But the relationship of each of those words to "expectation" is slightly different, and only one is *most* similar to the relationship between "cultivate" and "nurture." This tests our reasoning by asking us to decide what is relevant and to provide deeper analysis than just connecting two alike things.

The Power of Words

Analogies show us how powerful words can be by showing us that two seemingly alike words can, in a certain context, create completely different results. Two synonyms may appear to be equal in meaning, but upon closer inspection, have a number of subtle differences that can make a world of difference in certain circumstances … such as your grade on an analogy test. In a way, the power words hold is incredible; it gives us the means to express ourselves in nearly unlimited ways. But at the same time, with so many options, it can be difficult to pick the right ones.

Critical thinkers know well how much words matter. When properly selected, they can clearly define or articulate discoveries, ideas, and inquiries that allow us to formulate our thoughts into concepts. But there are often several possible meanings for a single word and even more for a sentence or a paragraph. Therefore, choosing the words for posing arguments is a task that should be considered carefully.

Immanuel Kant, a revered critical thinker, felt that analogies were the fruits of creative thinking. But others, like English philosophers John Locke and Thomas Hobbes, were hesitant of the inherent ambiguity they held. Analogies were not just straightforward word puzzles—they were difficult tests of our ability to make connections. And we weren't always right. Although Hobbes and Locke acknowledged that analogies had their time and place and could be used to develop our thinking skills and communication, there was just too much room for error when it came to word choice. This may not be a big deal when it comes to testing ourselves about the connection between everyday tools and types of instruments, but it becomes a real issue when explaining complex topics.

When you start to look for analogies, you'll see them, not just on your school assessments, but everywhere. Writers love analogies, also known in literature as similes and metaphors. People also often lean on analogies to teach or explore ideas. In fact, I've used a number of them in this book! When used in the right way, these comparisons can allow us to demonstrate an unfamiliar idea with more familiar terminology or stress the importance or deeper meaning of something. But because these connections require so much creative and critical thinking, they can often be misunderstood and may be lost in translation. Whether an analogy will be successful or not comes down to picking the right words. And that's no easy feat.

Words are tricky. We may assume we are communicating with others in a perfectly straightforward and simple manner only to find out that the message we were attempting to convey was not the message that was received by the listener. Ever played a game of telephone? You may think the word you're whispering into your neighbor's ear is clear as day. You know the sounds and the intention you're trying to convey. Still, "tomato" turns into "scuba diver" over the course of twenty or so whispered transmissions.

Not only can accents, tone, and context make a difference in a word's meaning, but so can intention and emotion. Words are not always black and white. All of these variables color a word in a particular way for that particular sentence, moment, and feeling. For example,

"YES!" is very different when expressed as "Yes?" or even "Yes." and is used very differently. One is an exclamation, the next an answer to a call, and the third a simple confirmation that, depending on the speech, could be bland and boring or sarcastic. "Yes" is just a three-letter word, but it can have a million meanings depending on the intonation it's expressed with.

The history and context of a word can also be of great importance. For example, let's look at the word "happiness." Happiness seems like a relatively simple-to-grasp feeling and word with a straightforward definition. Yet, Thomas Jefferson and the founding fathers felt so strongly about it that they included it as an unalienable right: "life, liberty, and the pursuit of happiness."

But what does happiness mean? And what does it look and feel like? That we have the right to smile? The right to live with wild abandon? Some may say that the right to happiness means doing whatever the heck they want to do ... as long as it doesn't make someone else unhappy, that is. Politically, that's called libertarianism.

If I decide to populate my garden with ugly garden gnomes, why shouldn't I? It's not hurting anyone. This may make sense when it comes to things like your own garden, but having the freedom to do as you please could quickly get out of control. Destroying property, harming others, and stealing are just a few examples of unacceptable activities that the founding fathers did not intend to grant freedom to. But they weren't expressly stated and can, therefore, be debated.

Even a word as simple and harmless as happiness can be open to a variety of interpretations, leading to unintended problems. As critical thinkers, it is essential that we not only take into account the literal definition of a word but also carefully examine the context in which it is used in order to determine the meaning behind it.

Uncovering False Analogies

Although analogies can certainly be helpful, they can also be used to manipulate us, such as through marketing. Advertisers don't use analogies in such a tangible way as we've explored above, but through imagery, feelings, and associations, making them harder to spot. They use these techniques to create a sense that connections exist between two unalike things that aren't related to each other at all. For example, a TV ad may show images of happy smiling people taking supplements, causing our brains to make the connection between being happy with taking the supplement for sale on the screen ... even if the medication has nothing to do with mood.

Luckily, once you understand the place of false analogies in daily life, you will start to see through them. By improving your critical thinking, you'll start to naturally question how these connections are being made and whether they have a basis in fact or in false emotional feeling.

Analogy in Practice

Analogies aren't just helpful for explaining, but for discovering and experimenting. For example, physicist Niels Bohr came up with a hypothesis in 1920. He stated that a subatomic particle may behave in contradictory ways at the same time depending on whether or not it was being observed. He thought that these particles exist in every possible state at the same time, but when observed, and only then, are forced to take one state. In other words, he thought that subatomic particles simultaneously exist and don't exist.[45]

If that sounds like a weird concept to you, you'd be in agreement with Nobel Prize-winning theoretical physicist Erwin Schrödinger. In 1935, Schrödinger came up with a hypothetical experiment to disprove Bohr, which you may be familiar with. Schrödinger's cat tested Bohr's hypothesis by putting an imaginary cat, hammer, a bottle of poison gas, a radioactive atom, and a Geiger counter in a sealed box for an hour. The idea was that if the atom decayed within that time,

---

[45] Faye, Jan. Copenhagen Interpretation of Quantum Mechanics. Stanford Encyclopedia of Philosophy. 2014. https://plato.stanford.edu/entries/qm-copenhagen/

it would emit a particle that would cause the Geiger counter to trigger the hammer to break open the bottle of poison gas and kill the cat. Statistically, the atom had a 50/50 chance of decaying, meaning there was no way to know without looking in the box whether the cat was alive or dead and there was an equal probability of either being true. Therefore, the conclusion was that the cat was both dead and alive at the same time (exist and not exist) because nobody could observe it and know it for sure without looking.[46] Yet, no cats had to be harmed for the experiment to work.

Incredible discoveries were made, yet no real experiments were done. Schrödinger and Bohr simply used their abilities as critical thinkers to answer their questions through the power of

---

[46] IFL Science. Schrödinger's Cat: Explained. IFL Science. 2018. https://www.iflscience.com/physics/schrödinger's-cat-explained/

their own reasoning and the incredibly helpful tool of analogies.

Reflection: Practice Your Analogy Skills

Practice your own analogy skills by assessing these analogical arguments presented by the Middle Way Society:

1. Cars are responsible for killing and injuring people just like guns. If you believe guns should be restricted because they are deadly weapons, then you should favor restrictions being placed on cars too.

2. If you are driving and someone is killed because of your reckless driving, you should face the possibility of a life sentence just like a murderer would. In both cases, the outcome is the same—a person died.

3. Annually, fewer people die from using ecstasy than from riding horses. Since taking ecstasy is less dangerous than riding a horse, ecstasy shouldn't be illegal because riding a horse isn't illegal.

4. Some cultures practice arranged marriage. They defend the practice as being necessary since young people don't have the experience needed to wisely choose a partner. Even though they do not support arranged marriages, many people in Western culture use dating agencies or websites to select a partner. It is hypocritical for people who participate in those services to criticize the practice of arranged marriage.[47]

On the surface, these statements have a natural and logical flow, yet I'm sure something

---

[47] Ellis, Robert M. Critical Thinking 12: Analogies. Middle Way Society. 2014.
http://www.middlewaysociety.org/critical-thinking-12-analogies/

within you had a gut reaction of disagreement to at least one of them. Everyone uses overgeneralizations or gaps in information, which might have come to mind as you itched to debate it.

You know these aren't true because of your experiences, but what if you didn't know anything about the topics being discussed? Imagine you had never heard of ecstasy or horses. You might think that ecstasy being legal seems like a fine idea. Better yet, imagine this fact was told to you by someone who is an expert in ecstasy and horses. You would assume you should probably believe them. Wouldn't you? After all, you know nothing about horses or ecstasy, and they have a PhD in both subjects. They must know something you don't, and they appear to be a reliable source to take your information from.

This kind of reasoning takes place all the time around us, it's just not as obvious when it's on a subject we don't know much about or when it's presented by people we trust. It's easy enough to fall into the trap of trusting this type of reasoning. But to avoid it, all we must do is ask someone else or look at further research. And ask lots of questions, of course.

Even if you didn't know what ecstasy or horses were, if you asked "What are those things?" and the expert told you that one is a drug and one is an animal, you might start to wonder how there could be a connection. You would almost immediately lose confidence in what you were being told and start searching for further resources.

This is how we should approach most things in life, even when they are not so obviously incorrect to us.

Conclusion

We reached the end of our journey, my dear reader. I hope that by this point, you are more equipped with the basics of critical thinking. This book provided you with a good primer to adopt the skill. Remember, all the advice in the world won't change much in your life as long as you don't take action and start practicing what you learned.

I invite you to give yourself thirty days to deepen your critical thinking skills. Each day you ask yourself – and answer - one question, or do one practice you learned in this book.

Repetition, after all, is the mother of knowledge. Wherever you put your attention, that part of you will grow. Likewise, if you emphasize developing critical thinking skills, you will inevitably get better at it. But don't take my word for it. Experiment and experience it yourself. Please question everything you read in this book. Find your own path.

Best of luck.

A. R.

Summary Guide

Chapter 1: What Is Critical Thinking?

Thinking critically can improve your life in so many areas. Research has shown that those who are better critical thinkers can make connections between ideas in ways that other people cannot and judge the importance and significance of ideas more easily.[48] They are also more efficient at identifying quality arguments and evidence and can find errors in reasoning, whether it be their own or others, making them more likely to succeed and less apt to grow frustrated by challenges.

---

[48] Thinking, Critical. An Interview with Linda Elder About Using Critical Thinking Concepts and Tools. Critical Thinking. 2002. https://www.criticalthinking.org/pages/an-interview-with-linda-elder-about-using-critical-thinking-concepts-and-tools/495

Critical thinking can even promote creativity because it teaches you the importance of thinking in new ways and relying on the power of your own mind rather than accepting things as they are. Also, it relies on questioning ideas and looking at the bigger picture, which are often a part of the artistic process.

Chapter 2: Why Is Critical Thinking So Challenging?

Our minds are made to think, but the *way* they think can be altered with practice. Because stereotypes and biases are a way of shortcutting our thinking, our brains see them as the more efficient thought process and will rely heavily on them when left to their own devices. In comparison, research, skepticism, formulating questions, and other aspects of critical thinking take much more brain power and require our minds to work harder. To our minds, this is like deciding between going on a short walk or taking on a marathon.

Chapter 3: The Essentials Of Critical Thinking

The 7 Steps to Better Critical Thinking:

- Step 1. Question (Almost) Everything
- Step 2. Articulate the Question
- Step 3. Examine Evidence and Biases
- Step 4. Don't Let Emotional Reasoning Hold You Back
- Step 5. Avoid Overgeneralization
- Step 6. Think Again
- Step 7. Accept Uncertainty

Chapter 4: Why Critical Thinking Is So Hard: Emotions, Assumptions, And Biases

When someone asks us what we think about something, we often answer with how we feel rather than with logical statements. This is an unconscious and unintentional part of our intuition that recognizes an answer must be found quickly and reaches for the thing that's closest and easiest to grab.

Our desire for the world to make sense often wins out against our desire to be right. We piece together gaps in our knowledge by creating stories and beliefs so that we don't have to face the unknown.

By educating yourself about forms of common biases, you can start to see how they emerge in other people's attitudes and marketing, but also yourself. This awareness can help you establish tools for minimizing your reliance on them, allowing you to be less partial and more open-minded, making you a better critical thinker.

Chapter 5: How To Understand More Deeply

Anything you learn comes down to just a few basics that made up your early education. Whether it was learning your sight words and multiplication tables or how to ride a bike as a child, it opened up a whole new world.

Once you've mastered the fundamentals, you'll find yourself leaning on those core concepts as you're presented with more difficult stages.

Ask:

- What went wrong?
- What can you learn from your mistakes?
- What can you do differently in the future?

Check:

- Why did this work?
- How can it be repeated in the future?
- What went right?

Chapter 6: Reasoning By Analogy

Analogies compare two unlike things to highlight a connection that may not be obvious, leading us to consider how dissimilar things have similarities. By strengthening this muscle in our mind, we can start to see how things are associated in our reasoning and lead us to better understand how concepts relate.

Critical thinkers know well how much words matter. When properly selected, they can clearly define or articulate discoveries, ideas, and inquiries that allow us to formulate our thoughts into concepts.

Before You Go…

I would be so very grateful if you would take a few seconds and rate or review this book on Amazon! Reviews – testimonials of your experience - are critical to an author's livelihood. While reviews are surprisingly hard to come by, they provide the life blood for me being able to stay in business and dedicate myself to the thing I love the most, writing.

If this book helped, touched, or spoke to you in any way, please leave me a review and give me your honest feedback.

Thank you so much for reading this book! Don't forget to claim your free gift:

Visit www.albertrutherford.com to claim your FREE GIFT: The Art of Asking Powerful Questions in the World of Systems

References

Barton Swaim (11 March 2016). "'Trust, but verify': An untrustworthy political phrase". The Washington Post. Retrieved 25 June 2019.

Biswas-Diener, Robert. Kashdan Todd B. What Happy People Do Differently? Psychology Today. 2013. https://www.psychologytoday.com/us/articles/201307/what-happy-people-do-differently

Brainy Quote. Thomas A. Edison. Brainy Quote. 2021.

https://www.brainyquote.com/quotes/thomas_a_edison_109004

Brogaard, Berit. PhD. Linda The Bank Teller Case Revisited. Psychology Today. 2016. https://www.psychologytoday.com/us/blog/the-superhuman-mind/201611/linda-the-bank-teller-case-revisited

Burger, E. B., & Starbird, M. P. (2012). The 5 elements of effective thinking. Princeton University Press.

Correia, Vasco. Biases and fallacies: The role of motivated irrationality in fallacious reasoning. Vasco Correia. 2018.
https://pdfs.semanticscholar.org/7f27/529ac93c3d86bd2b251d1787c63f0d10fb3c.pdf

Dunning, D., Meyerowitz, J., & Holzberg, A. Ambiguity and Self-Evaluation: The Role of Idiosyncratic Trait Definitions in Self-Serving Assessments of Ability. In T. Gilovich, D. Griffin, & D. Kahneman (Eds.), Heuristics and Biases: The Psychology of Intuitive Judgment (pp. 324-333). Cambridge: Cambridge University Press. doi:10.1017/CBO9780511808098.020. 2002. https://www.cambridge.org/core/books/heuristics-and-biases/ambiguity-and-selfevaluation-the-role-of-idiosyncratic-trait-definitions-in-selfserving-assessments-of-ability/AD02843FDFE75A167603DA6469565562

Elder, Linda. Paul, Richard. The Analysis & Assessment of Thinking. Critical Thinking. 2017.
http://www.criticalthinking.org/pages/the-analysis-amp-assessment-of-thinking/497

Elder, Linda. Paul, Richard. Universal Intellectual Standards. Critical Thinking. 2017. http://www.criticalthinking.org/pages/universal-intellectual-standards/527

Ellis, Robert M. Critical Thinking 12: Analogies. Middle Way Society. 2014. http://www.middlewaysociety.org/critical-thinking-12-analogies/

Faye, Jan. Copenhagen Interpretation of Quantum Mechanics. Stanford Encyclopedia of Philosophy. 2014. https://plato.stanford.edu/entries/qm-copenhagen/

Frank, T. What is Critical Thinking? - Definition, Skills & Meaning. Study. 2018. http://study.com/academy/lesson/what-is-critical-thinking-definition-skills-meaning.html

Goodreads. Socrates. Goodreads. 2021. https://www.goodreads.com/quotes/738227-one-thing-only-i-know-and-that-is-that-i

IFL Science. Schrödinger's Cat: Explained. IFL Science. 2018. https://www.iflscience.com/physics/schrödinger's-cat-explained/

Insight Assessment. Expert Consensus on Critical Thinking. Insight Assessment. 2018. https://www.insightassessment.com/Resources/Importance-of-Critical-Thinking/Expert-Consensus-on-Critical-Thinking

Kahneman, Daniel. Thinking, Fast and Slow. Penguin. 2011.

Literary Devices. To Thine Own Self Be True. Definition and Examples of Literary Terms. 2021. https://literarydevices.net/to-thine-own-self-be-true/

Mages Blog. Hit and run. Think Bayes! Mages Blog. 2014. https://magesblog.com/post/2014-07-29-hit-and-run-think-bayes/

New Mexico Media Literacy Project. The Language of Persuasion. New Mexico Media Literacy Project. 2007. https://www.greenwichschools.org/uploaded/faculty/maryellen_brezovsky/CMS/8_Media_Literacy/The_Language_of_Persuasion.pdf

O'Reilly, Kim. PhD. Why Critical Thinking Is So Important. Intercultural Solutions. 2008. https://www.interculturalsolutions.net/why-critical-thinking-is-so-important/

Quotemaster. Flattery will get you everywhere. - Mae West. Quotemaster. 2021.

https://www.quotemaster.org/q825fde4a9be73cd0d44d44bbe05a2c8d

Shea, Brendan. Karl Popper: Philosophy of Science. Internet Encyclopedia of Philosophy. 2018. https://www.iep.utm.edu/pop-sci/

Soll, Jack B. Milkman, Katherine L., Payne, John W. A User's Guide To Debiasing. 2018. http://www.opim.wharton.upenn.edu/~kmilkman/Soll_et_al_2013.pdf

St. B. T. Evans, Jonathan & L. Barston, Julie & Pollard, Paul. On the Conflict between Logic and Belief in Syllogistic Reasoning. Memory & cognition. 11. 295-306. 10.3758/BF03196976. 1983. https://www.researchgate.net/publication/16575665_On_the_Conflict_between_Logic_and_Belief_in_Syllogistic_Reasoning

Tarvis, Carole, and Carol Wade. *Psychology in Perspective,* 2nd ed. (Longman Publishers,

1997);Wade, Carole. Tavris, Carol. Gary, Marianne. Psychology, 5th ed. (Longman Publishers. 1998).

Thinking, Critical. An Interview with Linda Elder About Using Critical Thinking Concepts and Tools. Critical Thinking. 2002. https://www.criticalthinking.org/pages/an-interview-with-linda-elder-about-using-critical-thinking-concepts-and-tools/495

Thinking, Critical. Critical Thinking: Where to Begin. Critical Thinking. 2017. http://www.criticalthinking.org/pages/critical-thinking-where-to-begin/796

Thinking Writing. Non-Critical And Critical Approaches. Thinking Writing. 2018.

http://www.thinkingwriting.qmul.ac.uk/noncritical/critical

Wade, Carole. Tavris, Carol. Gary, Marianne. Psychology. Longman Publishers. 1998.

Walter, Ekaterina. Fail Your Way To Amazing Things. Forbes. 2013. https://www.forbes.com/sites/ekaterinawalter/2013/10/29/fail-your-way-to-amazing-things/#c92e41167596

Westside Toastmasters. Intellectual Humility. Westside Toastmasters. 2018. http://westsidetoastmasters.com/resources/thinking_tools/ch03lev1sec3.html

Westside Toastmasters. Intellectual Courage. Westside Toastmasters. 2018. http://westsidetoastmasters.com/resources/thinking_tools/ch03lev1sec4.html

Westside Toastmasters. Intellectual Autonomy. Westside Toastmasters. 2018. http://westsidetoastmasters.com/resources/thinking_tools/ch03lev1sec9.html

Westside Toastmasters. Intellectual Integrity. Westside Toastmasters. 2018. http://westsidetoastmasters.com/resources/thinking_tools/ch03lev1sec6.html

Westside Toastmasters. Intellectual Perseverance. Westside Toastmasters. 2018. http://westsidetoastmasters.com/resources/thinking_tools/ch03lev1sec7.html

Westside Toastmasters. Confidence in Reason. Westside Toastmasters. 2018. http://westsidetoastmasters.com/resources/thinking_tools/ch03lev1sec8.html

Westside Toastmasters. What does fair mindedness requires? Westside Toastmasters. 2018.

http://westsidetoastmasters.com/resources/thinking_tools/ch03lev1sec2.html

www.ingramcontent.com/pod-product-compliance
Lightning Source LLC
Chambersburg PA
CBHW072028230526
45466CB00020B/1078